Palgrave Socio-Legal Studies

Series Editor
Dave Cowan
University of Bristol Law School
Bristol, UK

"Naomi Creutzfeldt breathes new life into ADR scholarship, and in particular into our understanding of the limits, and potential, of the ombud institution. Combining ground-breaking empirical research in the UK and Germany with startling theoretical insight, she cogently demonstrates how our perceptions of what counts as fairness in an ADR context is decisively shaped by national legal culture. Local legal consciousness and socialization are thereby exposed as the determinants of trust, and national conceptions of legality as the conditions of informal justice. This formidable study stands, therefore, as an exemplar of the interdisciplinary approaches and methodological pluralism the author herself advocates if we are to identify new forms of legal consciousness, more trustworthy forms of ADR, and, despite national differences, a genuinely transnational ADR space. Law's conceptual empire, though still bedecked in much of its formal majesty, will rest less securely as a result of this searching interrogation of the informal ways and means of eluding its grasp."

—Dr. Nick O'Brien, Hon. *Research Fellow, School of Law and Social Justice, University of Liverpool, UK*

"Dr. Creutzfeldt is the undisputed expert on ombuds practice in Europe. Her pioneering research combines qualitative and quantitative analysis to provide tremendous insight into the ways in which individuals experience the ombuds system, as well as the broader implications of their experiences. This book is a must-read for anyone interested in the present and the future of ADR systems."

—Professor Rebecca Hollander-Blumoff, *Washington University, St. Louis, USA*

"The ADR Directive created a legal guarantee for consumers to access an 'informal justice system'. The aim is to increase consumer confidence in the market and to contribute to the standardization of the European internal market. This book addresses a shortcoming in the legislative process: it provides empirical data on consumers' knowledge of alternative dispute resolution and their assessment. The country comparison also shows how social, cultural and legal peculiarities affect the willingness to use ADR. The author's carefully designed fieldwork, as well as the lessons learned and conclusions, make a substantial contribution to understanding the importance and necessary development of alternative legal protection—issues that are also relevant in the context of Brexit."

—Prof. Dr. Günter Hirsch, *Insurance Ombudsman, former President of the Supreme Court of Germany and former Judge of the European Court of Justice*

The Palgrave Socio-Legal Studies series is a developing series of monographs and textbooks featuring cutting edge work which, in the best tradition of socio-legal studies, reach out to a wide international audience.

More information about this series at
http://www.palgrave.com/gp/series/14679

"Consumer ADR remains under-researched and especially empirical insights are missing. This leads to the omission of important themes in the discourse. It is thus determined by unrealistic fears rather than actual experiences. Naomi Creutzfeldt sheds some light into the dark with her study. The design of her study is impressive and the amount of responses allows for valuable insights: around 3.500 consumers reported their experiences with 14 different ADR providers.The differentiated results are of great value for practitioners for two reasons. First, they offer important feedback for the improvement of procedures and second, they offer convincing arguments for consumer ADR and its acceptance. Creutzfeldt's study provides a new quality of discussion to be had about consumer ADR and is highly recommended for both practice and academia!"

—Dr. Christof Berlin, *Head of Aviation, Conciliation Body for Public Transport*

"How people experience Alternative Dispute Resolution processes is likely to become an increasingly important question in the coming years, as social complexity and constraints on public funds necessitate the search for alternatives to existing legal frameworks. In this timely, comprehensive and accessible book, Dr. Creutzfeldt explores the wants, needs and assessments of the users of Ombudsman services in Germany and UK. Yet she does much more than this. By drawing out the links - and tensions - between two major bodies of theory and research, procedural justice theory and the concept of legal socialization, she shows how the seemingly universal concern for fair process among the users of legal services is mediated and moderated by first, a strong concern with outcomes, and second the legal culture within which people are socialized and which shapes their understandings of the processes and procedures used by legal actors. This book should be of interest to scholars working in both these fields, as well as practitioners across the whole range of public and private bodies seeking to improve existing, or institute new, ADR structures."

—Ben Bradford, *Professor of Global City Policing, UCL Jill Dando Institute of Security and Crime Science*

"Naomi Creutzfeldt is a fine scholar whose research has relevance and resonance across the academic/practitioner divide. Her pioneering work on public attitudes to public trust in a range of ombudsman services is characterized by rigour, accessibility of style, and strong comparative analysis. It is rare for scholarly work to be enthusiastically debated in ombudsman circles, but Creutzfeldt's writing constitutes an important set of considerations for the ombudsman and administrative justice communities."

—Rob Behrens, *Parliamentary and Health Service Ombudsman*

Naomi Creutzfeldt

Ombudsmen and ADR

A Comparative Study of Informal Justice in Europe

palgrave
macmillan

Naomi Creutzfeldt
University of Westminster
London, UK

Palgrave Socio-Legal Studies
ISBN 978-3-030-07653-5 ISBN 978-3-319-78807-4 (eBook)
https://doi.org/10.1007/978-3-319-78807-4

Cover credit: Digital Vision iii/Alamy Stock Photo

Printed on acid-free paper

This Palgrave Macmillan imprint is published by the registered company Springer International Publishing AG part of Springer Nature
The registered company address is: Gewerbestrasse 11, 6330 Cham, Switzerland

Foreword

In this important book, *Ombudsmen and ADR: A Comparative Study of Informal Justice in Europe*, Naomi Creutzfeldt has provided us with one of the first efforts to understand the meaning of "justice" in non-judicial settings across different legal systems. In seeking to understand how "alternative" (or as we say now, "appropriate") dispute resolution processes are being utilized in consumer disputes in Europe, in the forms of both public and private Ombudsmen, Naomi Creutzfeldt has learned that attitudes toward informal justice are inextricably connected to how we are socialized in our home jurisdictions to expectations of legality and justice. Her data and conclusions in this book will have far-reaching impacts on the socio-legal study of dispute resolution and how ordinary people understand their possibilities in seeking legal redress and also on policy initiatives and dispute system design as Europe continues to attempt to perfect a single market consciousness for trading across borders.

In a study that combines quantitative and qualitative measures, Naomi looks at how users of Ombudsman services in private sectors (telecom, energy, financial services, transport) and public settings (health care, public services) view the efforts of non-legal third-party dispute "resolvers" to help them manage disputes about billing, delays in services, and other disputes. Ombudsmen, originating in an older Scandinavian form of dispute resolution for management of grievances for governmental maladministration, has now been expanded to include neutral, third-party "helpers" of consumers, of both public services and private products and services in freestanding institutions of consumer redress. These newer Ombudsman institutions (some sector based; others more general) are one prominent form of dispute resolution (ADR) that has emerged from the Directives of the European Union requiring member states to provide expeditious forms of dispute resolution for transborder consumer transactions (EU Directive 2013/11 on consumer ADR and EU Regulation No. 524/2013 on ODR; see also EU Directive 2008/52/EC on use of mediation in cross-border commercial transactions).

The data presented in this book demonstrate that differences in the legal systems of the UK and Germany have marked efforts to create dispute systems outside of the legal system. We learn that in Germany the Ombudsmen services are hierarchical, managed by judges and lawyers, while those in the UK are more flexible and employ staff who are not necessarily legally trained. Users of the Ombudsman services demonstrate their expectations are based on their socialization within their own legal systems. Germans value fair outcomes and want payment and redress. Users from the UK value process fairness and want to express their "voice" in efforts to prevent bad things from happening to other people.

The data and the arguments presented in this book draw on well-established and traditional concepts in socio-legal studies, procedural justice, legal consciousness, and legal socialization, but their application to the new processes of "ADR" presents important new findings. Procedural justice may not be the controlling value in one-off, briefer encounters in seeking legal redress. When dispute resolution is by telephone or now, increasingly online, *outcome*, not "fairness, being heard" *process*, may be more important in some settings. This is an important finding and a direct challenge to many conventional claims about the importance of "procedural justice." As any good socio-legal scholar can recognize, settings and processes may change what is valued. It is the variations, as well as the "uniformities," in human behavior that we are interested in studying.

The findings of this superb research project have enormous implications for how we are currently reimagining how dispute resolution and legal redress may be achieved. Naomi Creutzfeldt reveals that measuring the "justice" in ADR settings may not be the same as user satisfaction or experiences of "justice" in the court system—if outcomes matter more than process, what might that say about dispute system design? Further, if ordinary users of Ombudsman services bring their expectations of what they want from such a system, from their home legal systems, what does that say about efforts to create transnational dispute resolution mechanisms?

This book poses some important challenges for scholars and policy makers alike—does "ADR" need its own *raison d'etre* and claims for legitimacy and acceptability, separate from the formal legal system? How can such a "culture" of ADR be achieved across so many different processes (e.g., mediation, arbitration, Ombudsmen and other hybrids) and across different legal cultures in the European Union? Will ODR (online dispute resolution) suffer the same issues as being deracinated from particular legal systems, or will buying online create a new world of "settling online" without any need for grand theories of justification and legitimacy? If ADR and ODR have both been created to improve access to justice for those who cannot afford the formal legal system, do they reintroduce their own troubles in providing access to justice—digital literacy and tech/computer access (see Ken Loach's 2016 movie I, *Daniel Blake*)?

In my own work, I have argued for recognition for *process pluralism*, an acknowledgment that "one size will not fit all" disputes and remedial possibilities. Naomi Creutzfeldt has given us one of the first rigorous studies of how one form of dispute resolution, varied across geographical and subject-matter spaces, is actually perceived by its users. Whether the users see Ombudsmen as a new or better process or just another part of the larger inaccessible legal system remains to be seen. This important book suggests dispute system designers must study their systems empirically and consider whether new designs are actually meeting access needs, or merely recapitulating, in a new form, older forms of dissatisfaction with justice-granting institutions. As Naomi Creutzfeldt suggests, perhaps "justice" is too big a concept for a quick and simple settlement or readjustment of an energy bill or miscredited charge account. As she suggests in this book, ADR (and ODR) will have to create their own story and justifications from "inside out."

Irvine, CA, USA

Carrie Menkel-Meadow
Chancellor's Professor of Law
(and Political Science)
University of California
Irvine School of Law

Acknowledgements

I would like to thank the ESRC FRL for generous funding of my three-year research project (grant number ES/K00820X/1). It provided the space, time, and resources for me to be able to go out and continue to explore the world of ADR in Europe. This book is one of the outputs. Many thanks also to the Law Faculty in Oxford, the Centre for Socio-Legal Studies, and the Programme for Civil Justice Systems for institutional support.

Huge thanks are due to the many Ombudsmen and their teams who supported my project. Their trust in me and in my research methods opened up a space that had not been empirically explored by academics before. I was therefore able to understand people's encounters with ADR across sectors and countries better. Findings along with practical recommendations from my project report have since been implemented into Ombudsmen procedures.

I thank Ben Bradford for his support in making sense of the quantitative dataset and his willingness to stretch his expertise on procedural justice to Ombudsmen. The survey was developed with input from Ben, Nigel Balmer, and Rebecca Hollander-Blumoff. I thank them for their interest in, and support of, my project.

In keeping me on track with my writing, I thank Kirsten McConnachie. Her thoughtful feedback on many draft chapters as part of our writing exchange kept me accountable and motivated.

Marie Selwood I thank for being such a wonderful and flexible editor and for being encouraging.

Carrie Menkel-Meadow is an inspiration and amazingly supportive, thank you.

From the bottom of my heart, I thank Ian Loader for making me laugh and for taking the time to patiently engage in discussions about justice & ADR and for probing my arguments.

Finally, being able to find "extra time" to write this book, I have to thank Samuel for being a superstar and clocking far too many hours on devices.

Contents

List of Figures

List of Tables

1

Ombudsmen and Informal Justice

Introduction

This is a book about how ordinary people experience the informal justice system. Based on an original dataset of recent users of ombudsmen,[1] an institution of the informal justice system, the rapidly developing literature on procedural justice and legal consciousness is taken to a new place. In combining these theories, I offer a comparative understanding of informal justice systems that are now spreading rapidly across Europe.[2] This book explores consciousness around 'alternatives' to formal legality, as legality constructs ideas about justice. The argument set forth is that people's expectations of informal justice are rooted in practices of (national) legal socialization. Posing the question of how everyday assumptions about law and perceptions of fairness guide our expectations of informal justice, I argue that the relationships people have with the informal justice system are shaped by their experiences and preconceptions about how the (formal) legal system and its agents behave and fulfil that role. As a result, expectations of providers of informal justice are prone to being unrealistic.

[1] In recent years the terms Ombudsman, Ombud and Ombuds have all come to be used in the literature on this topic. I have in fact used Ombuds in other publications (Creutzfeldt and Bradford 2016, 2018; Gill and Creutzfeldt 2017). However, since the term Ombudsman is an old Norse word and the actual and well-understood name of the institution I am studying, I have opted for the sake of clarity to use the term Ombudsman (and the plural Ombudsmen) throughout the book.

[2] The term informal justice system is used here to draw a distinction between state-administered formal justice systems and non-state administered informal justice systems (Wojkowska 2006).

N. Creutzfeldt, *Ombudsmen and ADR*, Palgrave Socio-Legal Studies,
https://doi.org/10.1007/978-3-319-78807-4_1

This volume develops new insights into the growing field of alternative dispute resolution (ADR) in general and the role of ombudsmen in particular. ADR takes many forms and has a multitude of meanings in different contexts. Specifically, I will be examining an institution that provides ADR in the informal justice system—the ombudsman. The terms 'ombudsman' and 'ADR' are often used in the same breath, but they are not interchangeable. Ombudsmen are a form of ADR, but not all ADR providers call themselves ombudsmen (more on this in Chapter 2). As my unit of analysis, I examine users' perspectives towards different types of ombudsmen. Studying ombudsmen offers a window into larger questions to do with ADR and informal justice. Taking examples from the administrative justice and the civil justice systems, appropriate dispute resolution is explored through the experiences of users of these systems.[3]

The book offers fresh insights into sectoral, national and cultural approaches to dispute resolution. Ombudsmen in my project cover EU-wide regulated sectors: energy, telecoms and financial services, which allows for cross-country comparisons. In addition to the private ombudsman models, I included public ombudsmen in my study for two reasons: firstly, to add to the richness of comparative empirical data; and, secondly, for a more comprehensive representation of ombudsman models. The data gathered allows comparisons between public and private sector ADR bodies in the UK and provides an insight into patterns of national-specific disputing behaviours. The original project looked at 14 ADR providers in the UK, Germany and France. It transpired during the data-analysis that the French dataset did not provide enough comparable data so I decided to exclude France from the empirical analysis. This leaves the principal focus of the book on the UK and Germany.

This book is based upon a rich and original dataset of 2777 recent users of ombudsmen in Germany and the UK and explores how they experienced their interaction with institutions of the informal ADR system. This has not been done before. Making use of both quantitative and qualitative data, the book focuses on the divide between users' expectations on the one hand, and what an ADR (informal justice) system can reasonably deliver on the other. This is achieved by comparing users' expressed expectations from my

[3]This book is based on the discoveries of my project (2013–2016) on 'Trusting the Middleman: Impact and Legitimacy of Ombudsmen in Europe'. https://www.law.ox.ac.uk/trusting-middle-man-impact-and-legitimacy-ombudsmen-europe. This work was supported by the Economic and Social Research Council (ESRC FRL grant number ES/K00820X/1).

datasets with EU and national regulations that determine the authority of the ADR bodies.

Consumer ADR in Europe has been revolutionised as a result of two broad forces: first, the on-going crisis in funding of civil litigation through the courts, associated cuts in legal aid and increases in court and legal fees. Second, the adoption by the EU of consumer ADR as a principal mechanism for the resolution of consumer–trader disputes through the creation of a pan-EU network of consumer ADR bodies, and a cross-border online dispute resolution (ODR) platform. These latter developments are legislated for under Directive 2013/11/EU on consumer ADR and Regulation (EU) No 524/2013 on ODR. Despite the legislation being implemented quite recently, promising access to justice in the European single market, little is known about what users of this ADR system expect from it.

At the time of writing, a relevant topical issue from the perspective of this book is Brexit. On 23 June 2016 UK citizens voted in a referendum to decide whether to remain in or to leave the EU. Leave won by 52–48%. The referendum turnout was 71.8%, with more than 30 million people voting (Eidenmüller 2016).[4] What effect will this development have on ombudsmen and ADR in the UK? One can only speculate at this point. However, due to the fact that the ADR legislation has been adopted into national law and ADR bodies and the ODR platform are already established, it is unlikely that ADR will disappear. ADR has developed in the UK quite independently of the EU. Therefore, ADR will continue to grow within the dispute resolution system and assert its place. However, there will have to be UK-internal proposals on how to further develop ADR and to consider the relationships and agreements with other ADR providers regarding cross-border complaints. This will surely not be a priority in the complex negotiations ahead. Disentangling 43 years of agreements and treaties with the EU will take a significant amount of time. In the meantime, I trust that providing empirical evidence about people's expectations of and attitudes towards informal justice systems in different legal cultures might assist the debate.

[4]See also www.bbc.co.uk/news/uk-politics-32810887; and https://disputeresolutionblog.practicallaw.com/the-adr-directive-what-impact-has-it-had-so-far-and-how-would-the-adr-market-be-affected-by-a-brexit/.

Trusting the Middle-Man: Impact and Legitimacy of Ombudsmen in Europe

In this book I have set out to answer two main questions. What explains users' perceptions of fairness and trust vis-à-vis ombudsmen institutions? And how do cultural frameworks influence citizens' use of ombudsmen? In order to answer these questions, I have integrated two bodies of literature that rarely address one another: procedural justice and legal consciousness. These are brought together through the methodology: a combination of the large quantitative dataset (of responses to closed questions) on the one hand, and the richness of responses to the open-ended questions in the survey and interviews provided country specific narratives on the other.

The comparative strengths of qualitative and quantitative research methods matched the theoretical complexity of the study and helped establish empirical validity of the data. A structured case study comparison was conducted in two EU member state countries that were selected to represent diversity of cultural settings with respect to the rule of law: the UK and Germany. The data was collected through satisfaction surveys, focus groups, and semi-structured interviews. The survey was aimed at the target group of ombudsman users who have recently been through the complaints process. The development of the survey instrument was informed by focus groups, organized to bring together key stakeholders (ombudsmen, citizens' advice groups, and consumer associations). The survey was piloted before it went live. This approach was applied in both investigated countries to enable sensitivity towards the appropriate cultural and national-specific settings. The local ombudsmen sent out the survey to a random sample of their customers who had just been through their complaints procedure. As a follow-up to the survey, semi-structured interviews with users as well as ombudsmen in each location provided a richer understanding of people's perceptions, including the opportunity to explore further the cultural context.

The first question (about fairness perceptions) was based on quantitatively exploring procedural justice in a new context by measuring people's perceptions of an ombudsman procedure. This study is not looking at how public authorities or complained about bodies perceive the ombudsman. The focus is on the user of the system. The second question (about cultural frameworks), guided by qualitative considerations, uncovers differences in cultural approaches to ADR. The data suggest that the way people view ombudsmen is informed by their assumptions about legality, and I argue this is shaped by their legal socialization (Trinkner and Tyler 2016). The construction of legal attitudes reflects people's evaluations and expectations of a system and its institutions. Legal consciousness is explored in this context as an approach that helps to uncover cultural specificities (Merry 1990; Ewick and Silbey 1998; Halliday and Morgan 2013; Morgan and Kutch 2016).

People's expectations and acceptance of informal justice are based on experiencing a fair procedure (Tyler 2006). However, this is only one aspect of the complex set of expectations that condition people's relationship with informal justice. This experience is also informed by legal socialization through national and cultural contexts developed when growing up. Legal socialization influences how we expect legal authorities to make decisions, how those authorities should treat us, and lay beliefs about the boundaries of legal authority. In other words, although ADR is a system that provides informal dispute resolution, people who use this system do not share an *informal socialization* of the system and therefore exhibit distinct patterns of expectations of the system. These patterns are based on people's everyday encounters with and expectations of the formal legal system. This, I contend, is expressed and can be empirically explored through people's legal consciousness. The quality of the encounters with the informal system will have an impact on legitimacy of an ADR procedure and affect users' trust. Trust can be empirically understood as expectations about current and future behaviour—where positive experiences encourage trusting behaviour (Jackson and Gau 2016). In order to understand and comment on how trust can be built and maintained in an informal justice system it is necessary to unpack what users of that system expect and from where these expectations arise. In this book I shed light on how people who use ADR make sense of it and what this means for national and European informal justice.

Plan of the Book

Part 1: Setting the Scene

Chapter 2: Europe's Justice Systems

This chapter provides an overview of Europe's justice systems and introduces the consumer ADR directive and the regulation on ODR—these form the basis of the fundamental, EU-wide change to the informal dispute resolution landscape. It includes an outline of what the implementation of these new rules into national (UK and Germany) ADR infrastructure means for the justice systems. The implementation into national frameworks signifies different things in different jurisdictions and needs to be disentangled. I argue that, for the legitimacy of the new legislative framework for ADR/ODR to be accepted, it needs to be understood in a national context and through its relationship with the formal legal system.

Chapter 3: Models of Ombudsmen

In this chapter, I discuss the implementation of the consumer ADR directive in national legal spaces. This legislation is very recent and, most systems and their users still need to become aware of, and accustomed to, this developing regime. I argue that for ombudsmen to be accepted and trusted as part of a system of justice, they have to be understood in their national context. In so doing, I discuss the country case studies and highlight similarities and differences in the development of ADR bodies. I discuss national and cultural distinctions in the legal systems, as well as those between public and private ombudsmen. Every member state has its own traditions and legal systems that have formed their populations' approaches to disputes, attitudes to institutions and expectations of those institutions. I argue that the relationships we form with authorities influence the relationships discussed in this chapter: specifically, those between the citizen and the state and those between consumers and a business. These relationships are established and develop through our legal culture.

Chapter 4: Theorizing Procedural Justice and Legal Consciousness

In this Chapter, I introduce the theoretical and methodological approach. I start by discussing how the theory of procedural justice is brought to a new setting and how it requires an extended methodology to more fully understand what people expect from an ADR body. Here, legal socialization and legal consciousness are proposed as concepts to enhance the procedural justice findings in the data. The argument I advance in this chapter is that, to get a better understanding of people's expectations, attitudes, and perceptions of fairness towards/within a system of informal justice, a mixed-methods approach facilitates an examination of unexplored areas. This approach is able to provide a richer account of what is happening in everyday encounters with institutions of the informal justice system. In sum, this chapter lays out the theoretical and methodological considerations for the empirical evidence to follow in part two.

Part 2: Empirical Discoveries

Chapter 5: Expectations and Perceptions of Ombudsmen in a Cross-National Comparison

In this Chapter, I take the rich quantitative dataset and discuss people's attitudes towards an ombudsman. I show how these matter in relation to building trust and legitimacy in the ombudsman institution. Theories of procedural justice create the framework for the examination. Applied to a new context, the theory of procedural justice is critically analysed. I find that, despite the strong evidence on the importance of procedural justice to the legitimacy of authorities and resulting rule-abiding behaviour in this context, outcome also matters. I conclude by indicating the limits of the quantitative analytical framework and expand the inquiry through a qualitative layer that helps better understand respondents' self-reported perceptions. This leads into the argument of the next chapter: that legal socialization and legal consciousness explain what motivates people to think and act the way they do when interacting with a justice system.

Chapter 6: Everyday Assumptions about Ombudsmen

In this chapter, I introduce a further dimension to the analysis through the qualitative data. I suggest that we need to consider legal socialization and legal consciousness to get a better understanding of why we act the way we do when engaging with an ombudsman procedure. In a cross-cultural comparison, the ombudsman, as a model of justice, is explored. I argue in this chapter that people's relationship with the law plays a crucial part in how they negotiate their way through, and engage with, the informal system. To explore this proposition, the notion of legal socialization provides fertile ground when combined with the qualitative data. Here, narratives of legal consciousness are discussed. I explore how people's legal socialization and legal consciousness frames their understanding of an ombudsman procedure. I conclude that the formal legal system is likely to serve as a benchmark to shape attitudes towards the informal system.

Part 3: The Future of the Informal Justice System

Chapter 7: A European Informal Justice System?

In this Chapter, I question how we construct ideas of justice in ADR and ODR. The notion of an informal justice system is understood through the role the EU plays and the form of justice that ADR and ODR provide. Alongside this discussion, the concept of access to justice is revisited. I argue that there is no tangible system of informal justice in the EU. I explore how ADR as a model of justice can be meaningful and accepted throughout the EU if it is defined by its national implementation. I conclude that at present people are still negotiating the legitimacy of ADR/ODR and that the acceptance of ADR into everyday practice is far from visible.

Chapter 8: Growing Informal Justice

In this chapter, I argue that the development and proliferation of ADR in Europe for providing high-quality procedures and outcomes needs to be addressed from the inside-out. ADR, at its best, can contribute to access to justice and has the potential to be a model of dispute resolution that embraces users' notions of a just and fair procedure. ADR models then have to be designed to reflect values and ethical standards that go hand in hand with users' attitudes.

Does ADR (need to) create its own norms of fairness, justice and language? Thinking about justice, fairness, trust and legitimacy, questions guiding our future inquiries could include: do our traditional values and roles within our justice system have to be reconsidered? Do we need new measures and tools to create appropriate protection for actors and users in these new and rapidly growing spaces? How can we best understand these areas of little regulation and large complexity that cannot fully be captured by traditional methods, models and language?

Chapter 9: Paths for Theory and Research

In the conclusion, I briefly revisit my main argument that we need to grow and focus on ADR within the national cultural context and only then it might mature into a European space. I propose three areas that require more attention in the continued study of informal justice and ombudsmen in Europe. These are: the way in which ADR providers' systems are designed; the need to look out for vulnerable users; and the challenge of the digital.

Part I

Setting the Scene

2

Europe's Justice Systems

Introduction

Europe combines a collection of national justice systems (or legal traditions). For these systems to be measured for effectiveness, the EU Justice Scoreboard has been put in place to regularly evaluate these systems with reference to their timeliness, independence, affordability and user-friendly access.[1] They are applied not only to national court systems but also to alternative dispute resolution (ADR). One of the trends the scoreboards have shown is that ADR is incentivised and promoted in all member states. This ranges from civil and commercial to labour and consumer disputes. Generally speaking, ADR is recognized as a valid pathway to access justice in the European space. European legislators are therefore promoting ADR to support access to justice for consumers in the EU single market.

This chapter provides an overview of Europe's justice systems and introduces the consumer ADR directive and the regulation on online dispute resolution (ODR) these form the basis of the fundamental, EU-wide change to the informal dispute resolution landscape. This chapter includes an outline of what the implementation of these new rules into national (UK and Germany) ADR infrastructure means for the justice systems. This implementation into national frameworks means different things in different jurisdictions and needs to be disentangled for the empirical analysis to follow. Thus, in this chapter, I provide the context for my argument that,

[1] http://ec.europa.eu/justice/effectivejustice/files/justice_scoreboard_2016_en.pdf.

N. Creutzfeldt, *Ombudsmen and ADR*, Palgrave Socio-Legal Studies,
https://doi.org/10.1007/978-3-319-78807-4_2

Fig. 2.1 Justice systems—a basic overview placing informal dispute resolution into context

for the legitimacy of the new legislative framework for ADR/ODR to be accepted, it needs to be understood in a national context and through its relationship with the formal legal system.

Europe's Justice Systems

The term 'justice system' is understood here as an overarching framework of which the legal system is a part (see Fig. 2.1). A legal system is made up of an operative set of legal institutions, procedures and rules. It is a broad term that defines the laws we have, the processes for making those laws, and the processes for ensuring that the laws are followed. Our justice system reflects how people behave and how we (as a country) expect people, organizations and governments to behave towards each other. The institutions of any given justice system that are responsible for looking after citizens' grievances can generally be divided into those providing formal redress/solutions and those offering informal ones. The formal structure of the system to address people's grievances is made up of courts, judges, the police and prisons. Whereas the informal structure is made up of institutions that offer pathways to settlement combining various techniques of ADR (Creutzfeldt 2013).

The extent to which the informal ADR system is integrated alongside the formal legal system into the national justice system varies from country to country. To understand everyday social interactions with the justice system, the relationship between formal and informal needs to be unpacked in its national context. This chapter provides a brief overview of legal traditions and justice systems in Europe and then introduces EU legislation on ADR and ODR. This is the legal framework that underpins a developing European informal justice system.

Civil and Common Law Traditions

Broadly speaking in Europe there are two types of legal system—the common law and the civil law traditions—each with its own heritage (Stein 1992). The common law tradition developed in the Middle Ages in England and also applied in the British colonies (ibid.: 167). The civil law tradition developed in parallel in continental Europe and extended to the colonies of European imperial powers. The main differences are that the common law is uncodified. This means that it is largely based on judicial decisions on similar cases (precedent). These precedents are collated in collections of case law. Civil law, on the other hand, is codified. Each country's legal code exists in a continuous loop of updating and is specific to all matters that can be brought to a court (including procedure and punishment). These codes differentiate between different categories of law: procedural law, substantive law and penal law (Wranken 2015).

The UK has a common law tradition (Stein 1992; Lewis 1995; Pound 1999), whereas Germany has a civil law tradition (Groves 2017). Despite the different heritages of their legal systems, the countries examined in this book share broad classifications in their justice systems; these are criminal justice, administrative justice and civil justice.[2] The following analysis provides a basic overview of administrative and civil justice systems and their overall purpose. This sets the scene for the latter part of this chapter and the context of the book, namely, informal justice, ADR and ombudsmen—located in the administrative and civil justice systems.[3]

[2]For a detailed comparison of the various distinctions between these systems, see Head (2011).

[3]For the sake of completeness, I briefly outline the criminal justice system:

The criminal justice system is made up of a number of agencies, each responsible to a government department. These agencies typically are: legislative (law-making), police (law enforcement), adjudicative (courts) and corrective (prisons, probation, parole) (Dammer and Albanese 2010). The criminal

The Administrative Justice System

The administrative justice system also possesses its own set of institutions, rules and procedures. These are courts and tribunals, internal complaints reviews and ombudsmen. The administrative justice system (in its widest sense) can be defined as the 'combination of (1) initial decision-making by public bodies affecting people's rights and interests, including the substantive rules under which decisions are made, the procedures followed in making decisions; and (2) systems for resolving disputes relating to such decisions and for considering citizens' grievances' (Administrative Justice Steering Group 2009: 2).

Public bodies, including central and local government, make countless decisions every year that directly affect the lives of individual people. Administrative justice work focuses on fairness in the process for making these important decisions, the law that regulates public decision-making, and the ability to challenge public bodies that get it wrong (including ombudsmen, tribunals and courts).[4]

Mashaw (1983: 24) defines the administrative justice system as 'the qualities of a decision process that provide arguments for the acceptability of its decisions.' Adler (2006) provides an excellent account of its strengths and weaknesses and modifies Mashaw's model, with a focus on fairness and its meaning in the context of administrative decision-making. Adler also offers an extended analytical framework, based on empirical data (ibid.: 621ff). It is beyond the scope of this chapter to apply the models as analytical frameworks in this context. Rather my aim is to place the discussion about ombudsmen into the context of administrative justice.

The final report of the Administrative Justice Steering Group (2009: 2) states that:

---

legal system's aim is to punish wrongdoers for offences against society as a whole. If criminal justice is seen as a form of governance, its role involves imposing social order and acting as a mechanism for resolving disputes; it is also a technique for managing risk (Zedner 2004: 2). This system, like other systems, is built around a set of values and principles. The term 'criminal justice system' is also commonly used descriptively to refer to all those agents, institutions and practices entrusted with responding to crime. Broadly speaking, it concerns the relationships between the individual, the citizen and the state. The criminal justice system can be described as a 'dedicated form of justice that applies in relation to criminal cases as opposed to civil, family, or administrative matters – and that has its own laws, principles, rules, procedures, codes, practices and thinking' (Gibson and Cavadino 2008: 9).

[4]http://justice.org.uk/our-work/areas-of-work/administrative-justice-system/.

> The benefits of this broad definition [of administrative justice] are that it delimits a coherent field of inquiry and enables discussion of administrative justice to respond to the full range of citizens' concerns about their interaction with public services.

The report concludes by stating the aims of an administrative justice system to be threefold:

- ensuring public bodies get it right the first time when making decisions;
- ensuring that, where decisions are incorrect or treatment of citizens is otherwise defective, there are effective redress mechanisms; and
- ensuring that public bodies learn from their mistakes, increasing the likelihood of getting it right the first time (ibid.: ii).

Within the system of administrative justice, public sector ombudsmen typically recommend a course of action with a 'win–win' outcome in mind—a friendly solution. An ombudsman system can collect complaint data, detect systemic problems and provide feedback to the local authorities, central government and health authorities to keep them in check. Ideally, an ombudsman becomes a moral authority by being fair, independent and accepted by institutions and users. Generally speaking, as Gill (2011) finds, ombudsmen are now expected to play a more active role in improving administrative decision-making by helping public officials learn from their mistakes.

The Civil Justice System

Taken in its broadest sense, the aim of the civil justice system is to regulate relationships between individuals. Civil justice is a way for individuals to achieve a fair solution when they have been injured or harmed due to another person's negligence, recklessness, or malpractice. In other words, the civil justice system allows individuals to hold others accountable for their actions.[5] There are several avenues to do this. As Genn suggests: 'There are many stakeholders in civil justice systems and a wide variety of civil justice problems' (2010: 5). It is difficult to conceptualise civil justice systems, as compared to criminal justice systems (or administrative justice systems) because of their complexity and undefined margins. However, generally speaking, 'the machinery of civil justice sustains stability and economic

[5] http://study.com/academy/lesson/what-is-civil-justice-definition-process-rules.html.

growth by providing public processes for peacefully resolving civil disputes, for enforcing legal rights and for protecting private and personal rights' (Genn 2012: 3).

An important part of a civil justice system is concerned with everyday life, involving a rich and complex variety of problems. In this sense, the civil justice system 'has a significant social purpose and needs to deliver just outcomes by means of procedures that are fair and that are perceived to be so by its users, a system that delivers justice and enjoys public confidence' (Genn 2010: 78). This is where ADR enters the justice landscape: 'ADR is exciting in part because it allows and encourages us to move beyond our existing [formal legal] conceptions. Without abandoning what is precious about our legal system, we must also be open to new possibilities as we begin to rethink our approach to procedural justice' (Sternlight 2003: 304). Before embarking on the discussion of procedural justice (see Chapter 4), I will first clarify the institutions of the informal justice system in Europe with which this book is concerned.

Informal Justice and ADR

The ideal of informal justice has been described by Roberts and Palmer (2005: 10) as: 'non-bureaucratic, local, accessible for ordinary people, reliant on lay people as third party interveners, outside the immediate scope of official law, based on substantive and procedural "rules", intent on promoting harmony'. Informal justice, then, is aimed at resolving certain types of problems where institutions of the formal justice system are failing to provide effective remedies. This translates into the criteria against which institutions that provide informal justice are measured: timeliness and effectiveness; impartiality and independence. ADR as a form of informal justice is expected to deliver these measures in its procedures and its interactions with people using the system.

ADR, as part of the informal justice system, 'is not, an entirely separate legal order, rather it is an enclave within a broader culture in which liberal legal ideology is well institutionalised' (Sarat and Garth 1998: 17). I build on this notion to shape my understanding of ADR and informal justice as part of the overall system providing justice. It is a collection of mechanisms that provide ADR. They constitute an additional pathway for citizens/consumers to obtain information and advice, seek redress for their grievance, and ultimately come out of the process with a feeling of being treated fairly and better understanding the informal process towards dispute resolution (see Chapter 4). What makes understanding ADR more complicated is that it functions as an umbrella term that covers a variety of techniques and approaches to resolving disputes in all kind of different settings. How then is the appropriate approach chosen for a specific dispute resolution setting? Menkel-Meadow (2016) suggests that:

> … not every dispute or conflict should be handled in the same way, so we now talk of 'process pluralism.' Much of our choice about what is 'appropriate' depends on *who* we are having a conflict with (a friend, family member, stranger, the government, an organization, a number of parties, organizations or countries) and *what* the dispute is about (a scarce resource, like land or property or money, or something we could share, or something we want to do that is new rather than routine (for which we could use a formal contract).

Having briefly engaged with some of the complexities that ADR presents (terminology, understanding and context), I want now to do two things: first, to situate ADR (as part of the informal justice system) within the wider national justice system alongside the formal justice system; second, to narrow the ADR focus to problems people encounter with institutions in civil and commercial disputes (consumer to business) and administrative justice disputes (citizen and state). An ADR body that has proven to stand the test of time and cultural diversity is the 'ombudsman model' (Creutzfeldt 2018). This is the focus of study in this book and will provide a window into a broader understanding of the informal justice system.

ADR and the Ombudsman Context

One of the established models that provide ADR is the ombudsman (details of how these models differ and sit within their national architecture are discussed in Chapter 3). At this stage, thinking about justice systems, it is important to understand where the ombudsmen in this study are situated. Generally speaking public sector ombudsmen are found as part of the administrative justice system and private sector ombudsmen are part of the civil justice system (Seneviratne 2002; Buck et al. 2011; Hodges et al. 2012).

The boundaries between public and private ombudsmen can be blurry. Depending on what measures we choose, they could be based on the *functions* they carry out, their *powers*, their *jurisdictions*, or the *types of problems* they deal with. There can be many different answers and approaches to classifying this distinction, depending on the context. For the purpose of my study, the public–private divide follows the ADR/ODR legislation for private ADR providers in the civil justice system and public ombudsmen that are part of the administrative justice landscape in the UK (more in Chapter 3).

Despite the significance of ombudsmen to our constitutional and civil justice landscapes, little is known about users' perceptions of the fairness of procedures and practices, and the significance of these perceptions for levels of trust in particular ombudsman offices. This book makes a start on plugging these gaps.

The rapid expansion of the *ombudsman enterprise* across the public and private sectors (a phenomenon Harlow and Rawlings (2009) have termed *ombudsmania*) has brought with it a blossoming of institutional and jurisdictional arrangements, operational styles and decision-making processes (Pound 1906). Although this poses some challenges in conceptualising a unified ombudsman institution, it offers distinct advantages for the study of the relationship between decision-making practices on the part of ombudsmen, perceptions of procedural justice, and levels of trust on the part of users across different jurisdictions and cultures. The principal advantage is that this area of comparative ADR research is yet to be explored and this book offers a unique approach, and starting point, to understanding what users of ADR institutions expect.

One of the aims of ombudsmen is to create and sustain public trust in institutions of government (public ombudsmen) and in the marketplace (private ombudsmen). A lack of public trust has become a 'cliché of our times' (O'Neill 2002: 9). How can a body that provides informal dispute resolution also provide a remedy that builds trust? Public trust in the ombudsman, as Behrens (2015: 5) suggests, has four key elements (perceived honesty and independence, core competence in delivery of service, development of strong internal culture fostering standards, and establishing active trust and trustworthy behaviour by professionals. These chime in with procedural justice criteria (see Chapter 5). If these elements are successfully conveyed to a user of an ADR model then this will build trust in the system.

ADR is not a new approach. The notion of ADR has its roots in ancient traditions going back many centuries (Hodges et al. 2012). In fact, over time ADR has been prioritized within some civil procedure systems. In England and Wales, for example, ADR was given an institutional and functionally important position within civil procedure as a result of the Woolf Reforms of 1996,[6] implemented as of 1999.[7] Lord Woolf's review of the procedures and rules of the civil courts in England and Wales aimed to improve access to justice. He suggested this be done by three means: reducing the costs of litigation; simplifying the procedural rules and modernising terminology; and removing unnecessary complexities in the litigation process. In other words, this connected ADR with civil justice reform and thus with the formal framework of civil procedure (Jackson 2016). An additional EU-wide drive for integration of mediation into European civil procedure systems occurred through the Mediation Directive 2008/52/EC (Hopt and Steffek 2012). Its purpose is to build trust in the process of mediation within the EU. The directive notes a number of advantages of mediation over litigation, including that cost-effectiveness, flexibility and the fact that agreements reached through mediation are more likely to be adhered to voluntarily without further recourse to the courts.

Abraham (2008) argued that ombudsmen deserve to be seen as a system of justice in their own right, albeit one that is different from, but complementary to, the courts and tribunals. Whilst Abraham is referring to public sector ombudsman, the 'ombudsman brand' has also been imported into the private sector, which, in my opinion, has opened up an opportunity to merge the debate about ombudsmen and their overarching purpose (Creutzfeldt 2018).

In contrast, consumer ADR is not well known. As will be shown later in the book, consumer ADR has developed in its own unique space, with its own design. At its best, it is intended as a pathway to justice that provides remedies and redress for low-value consumer claims. As outlined in Chapter 3, ADR can take many forms and is used as an umbrella term to include many different models of dispute resolution. Consumer ADR is not a competitor or replacement of the courts; rather it is an added avenue for accessing justice (Creutzfeldt 2013, 2016). In other words, ADR is a dispute resolution model, aimed at settlement and designed for a particular type of dispute. The disputes I am focusing on are those of consumers and business in the private sector, as well as those between citizens and public authorities in the public sector.

Despite the differing nature of disputes brought to private and public ombudsmen (from overcharged utility bills to a wrongdoing in a nursing

[6]Woolf Reforms and the Civil Procedure Rules 1998. Accessed 15 November 2017. https://www.insolvencydirect.bis.gov.uk/technicalmanual/Ch13-24/Chapter19/part2/part_2.htm.

[7]Not to mention the whole process of tribunalisation in the early twentieth century.

home: see Chapter 3), they offer similar escalating procedural steps. These steps usually commence with a triage function at first contact (online platform, email or phone), where the admissibility of complaints is assessed. Many of the contacts are requests for information and are usually re-directed to the service provider about whom the complaint has been made, as their internal complaints process has to be unsuccessfully completed before the ombudsman can be involved. If a complaint is *ripe* and admissible to the ombudsman, then it travels through the various stages of investigation. At every stage the complaint handlers/case workers seek to find a settlement between the complainant and the service provider. The next stage is usually an early evaluation and possible resolution, mutually accepted settlement and as a final outcome an ombudsmen adjudication (Creutzfeldt 2014). The stage a complaint reaches varies according to the case dealt with and the type of ombudsman involved. Generally speaking though, most cases do not go as far as a final ombudsman decision, typically getting settled before that.[8] The ombudsman, as part of the legal system, provides another avenue to access justice (Seneviratne 2005: 181).

Access to Justice

Access to justice has emerged as a social right. According to Cappelletti and Garth (1978: 182) effective access to justice can be seen as the most basic requirement, the most basic human right of a system which purports to guarantee legal rights. This system must be equally accessible to all and lead to results that are individually and socially just. Put differently, effective access to justice can be considered as the most basic element of a system which promises to uphold legal rights.[9] Access to justice, therefore, is a complex matter and does not simply equate to legal aid, for example. 'Access to justice includes access to courts, lawyers, advice agencies, the police, and ombudsmen. It means public authorities behaving properly. It means everyone having some basic understanding of his or her rights. It means making law less complex and more intelligible' (Moorhead 2011).

The phrase 'access to justice' is a political, legal and rhetorical symbol of undeniable power and attractiveness (Cappelletti and Garth 1978; Cappelletti 1981). Cappelletti (1981) described access to justice as consisting

[8]See, for example, the annual reports of the various ombudsmen for more details and figures.

[9]http://justice.org.uk/our-work/areas-of-work/access-to-justice/.

of three waves of change, especially with a focus on its development in the USA (and most Western countries post-Second World War). The first wave contains reforming institutions to provide legal services for the poor (emergence of legal aid); the second wave extends representation to diffuse interests (consumers or environmentalists—collective rights); the third wave questions the effectiveness of dispute-resolving institutions and examines less formal alternatives to traditional courts—the emergence of a fully developed access to justice approach.

This book rides on the third wave and focuses on alternative pathways to dispute resolution. Wrbka (2015: 278) described 'access to justice 2.0' as 'the quest for a legal framework that tries to ensure that consumer interests are safeguarded to the best possible extent by identifying and implementing certain parameters.' EU-wide measures were taken to boost consumer confidence in the internal market, to encourage cross-border trade and promote access to justice. This led to the development of a new comprehensive approach to resolve problems in contemporary Europe through introducing consumer protection tools: the 'ADR directive' and the 'ODR regulation'.

The New Landscape of Civil Justice in Europe

European legislators frequently promote ADR to support access to justice for consumers in the EU single market (Hodges et al. 2012; Creutzfeldt 2013). The 2011 European Commission 'Special Eurobarometer'[10] reports that one in five consumers have encountered a problem with goods and services purchased in the EU; this adds up to a reported detriment of about 0.4% of EU gross domestic product. Most consumers complain to the traders but, if they are unsuccessful in getting their complaint resolved, they typically do nothing. Two recent pieces of EU legislation are intended to counter this trend and to encourage consumers to access justice more easily through ADR and ODR.

In 2013, European legislators passed the directive on consumer ADR (2013/11/EU) (the ADR directive) and the regulation on ODR (EU) 524/2013 (the ODR regulation).[11] Laying the foundations for the 2013

[10]European Commission, 'Special Eurobarometer 342: Consumer Empowerment' (2011): http://ec.europa.eu/public_opinion/archives/ebs/ebs_342_en.pdf.

[11]Directive 2013/11/EU of the European Parliament and of the Council of 21 May 2013 on alternative dispute resolution for consumer disputes, amending Regulation (EC) No 2006/2004 and Directive 2009/22/EC (Directive on Consumer ADR) [2013] OJ L165/63; Regulation (EU) No 524/2013 of the European Parliament and of the Council of 21 May 2013 on online dispute resolution for

legislation (without binding principles), two European Commission recommendations on ADR were passed in 1998 and 2001.[12] Then, in 2008, the mediation directive—aimed at court and extra-judicial proceedings—was passed.[13] Since then, ADR has developed at different speeds in different sectors, particularly in the regulated sectors (e.g. financial services, energy, telecoms) where ADR became compulsory, and it has encouraged the development of specialized networks (ECC-Net, FIN-Net).[14]

The consumer ADR directive ensures that consumers and traders can turn to an ADR entity for all their contractual disputes in virtually all economic sectors—except for healthcare and education—no matter where (domestically or across borders) and how (online/offline) the purchase was made. The ODR regulation aims at facilitating the use of ADR for disputes arising from online purchases (Cortes and Lodder 2014). The new legislation (implemented in 2015) was aimed at ensuring full ADR coverage, high quality ADR bodies, easy access to the right ADR body, and a means of submitting and resolving disputes online through an EU wide platform.[15] The current status of this ambitious legislation will be empirically explored in Chapters 5 and 6.

The new legislative framework aims to improve consumer protection and enforce consumer rights in the EU single market. Some commentators are doubtful of this soft law approach and claim it is aimed at ultimately

---

consumer disputes and amending Regulation (EC) No 2006/2004 and Directive 2009/22/EC (Regulation on consumer ODR) [2013] OJ L165/1.

[12]Commission Recommendation 98/257/EC of 30 March 1998 on the principles applicable to the bodies responsible for out-of-court settlement of consumer disputes. Commission Recommendation 2001/310/EC of 4 April 2001 on the principles for out-of-court bodies involved in the consensual resolution of consumer disputes [2001] OJ L 109/56.

[13]Directive 2008/52/EC of the European Parliament and of the Council of 21 May 2008 on certain aspects of mediation in civil and commercial matters [2008] OJ L 136/3.

[14]The year 2015 marked 10 years since the European Commission, together with national governments, established a network of European Consumer Centres (ECC) in all 28 member states of the European Union, Norway and Iceland (the ECC-Net). The ECC-Net promotes the understanding of EU consumers' rights and assists in resolving complaints about purchases made in another country of the network, when travelling or shopping online. 'European Consumer Centres' (European Commission: Consumers, 2015): http://ec.europa.eu/consumers/solving_consumer_disputes/non-judicial_redress/ecc-net/index_en.htm; 'Welcome to FIN-NET' (Financial Dispute Resolution Network): http://ec.europa.eu/finance/fin-net/index_en.htm.

[15]See the ODR platform: https://webgate.ec.europa.eu/odr/main/index.cfm?event=main.home.show&lng=EN.

Europeanising consumer law (Schulte-Nölke 2015). This is coupled with the fear of the reduction in the number of cases brought to courts (resulting in no case law) and a rush towards privatised justice (Eidenmüller and Engel 2014). These worries will be further considered in Chapter 6.

In the post-implementation period in which this book is being written, attention is paid to culture and the specific relationships and expectations that we have towards ADR procedures. This varies between some member states with an existing and developed ADR culture or socialization (see Chapter 3) and other member states where ADR is an unfamiliar (and therefore less trusted) approach (for an examination of the different implementation stages see Creutzfeldt 2015, 2016). One of the central claims I make in this book is that the distinct national context (legal system) in which ADR is situated will influence its acceptance. Therefore, despite its overarching goal of assisting people to access justice in the European space, we need to understand how institutions of the informal system are integrated and accepted at the national level.

The following section moves into the national space and provides an overview of the justice systems of the countries considered in this book: the UK and Germany. The focus here is to highlight relationships between the courts (representing the formal legal system) and ADR, thereby starting to tease out the cultural nuances that will be discussed in more detail throughout the next chapters as the book unfolds.

The Justice System in the UK

The UK has three jurisdictions: England and Wales, Scotland, and Northern Ireland. Her Majesty's Courts and Tribunals Service (HMCTS) is responsible for the administration of many of the courts in England and Wales. The HMCTS is an agency of the Ministry of Justice, the government department overseeing the justice system in England. Different courts are set up to hear different cases. Criminal cases in England and Wales are heard in the magistrates' courts, the Crown Court and the criminal division of the Court of Appeal. Civil cases in England and Wales are mainly heard in the county courts, the High Court and the civil division of the Court of Appeal, with magistrates' courts having jurisdiction for a range of applications made under various pieces of legislation. The UK Supreme Court is the final court of appeal in the UK for both criminal and civil cases, although this right of appeal does not apply to Scottish criminal cases.

Consumer claims are dealt with in civil courts and these are split into three tracks depending on the value of the claim.[16] For claims under the value of £10,000, the small claims track is available. For these cases consumers are usually not legally represented, preferring to bring a lay representative or represent themselves. There are costs involved and the small claims system is not as popular as was anticipated (Hodges et al. 2012). This is where ADR can become a very attractive alternative, especially since, after exhausting the ADR process, the path to court remains an option.

The courts in the UK that can be approached with consumer problems are known to be overstretched, have long waiting times, and are unpredictable in cost (legal representation), duration, and case outcomes (Hodges et al. 2012). In addition, taking a case to court amplifies the problem in a person's life in a way that is usually disproportionate to the value of the claim. Studies have shown that people do not go to a court for a dispute that is worth less than €500.[17] This means that low-value consumer complaints do not often find their way to court. This is one of the misconceptions about the ADR and ODR legislation—it does not aim to take cases away from the courts, rather it aims to provide additional pathways to justice for complaints that would otherwise not be heard.

The ADR landscape in the UK, as in other European member states, has transitioned into a regulated space since the implementation of the ADR directive into national law. There is a range of different ADR models (covering the regulated and unregulated sectors),[18] offering a variety of procedures and outcomes (Creutzfeldt 2016c). However, the bottom line is that, despite there being a wide offering of ADR methods, consumers remain either unaware of ADR or confused as to which provider is responsible for what. To ease consumer access to ADR, the UK was initially thinking about creating a single consumer ombudsman but this did not materialize due to competition amongst the existing ADR providers as to who might fill this role. The government decided to leave the market open for ADR providers to compete. This has now produced an ADR landscape in the UK that is not only difficult to impossible for consumers to navigate, but has also created a space for exploitation of the market.[19]

---

[16]Claims of up to £10,000 are put in the *small claims track*; claims of £10,000–25,000 are usually put in the *fast track*; claims over £25,000 are put in the *multi-track*.

[17]European Commission (Special Eurobarometer 342) consumer empowerment; available at: http://ec.europa.eu/consumers/consumer_empowerment/docs/report_eurobarometer_342_en.pdf.

[18]Regulated sectors: financial services, energy, legal services, aviation, rail, postal services and water. Unregulated sectors: second-hand cars, retail, property, travel and estate agents.

[19]For example: claims management firms, more than one ADR provider serving the same sector, and crossover in ombudsmen jurisdictions and responsibilities between sectors.

Citizens Advice

What does this mean for the users of ADR and the acceptance thereof? Well, as indicated above, although there is ample ADR provision available in the UK, it remains a challenge for the consumer to find it. Throughout the UK, Citizens Advice Bureaux[20]—a national charity—are the go-to point for ordinary people to find advice and help with their problems. It is a free service that provides confidential, independent and impartial advice to everyone about rights and responsibilities. The charity has 21,600 highly trained volunteers supporting the delivery of its work. Despite financial constraints and other challenges, Citizens Advice Bureaux throughout the country remain the intuitive access point for seeking advice and signposting to ADR providers. Here, more effort is needed to work together to improve the systems of signposting and communication.

A Nation of Moaners

The British are no natural complainers. Although I am briefly diverging into stereotypes, I believe it will assist the understanding of how national characteristics play a role in the use of dispute resolution systems. A common cliché about *Britishness* is a tendency for people to moan (to friends and colleagues) but not to actually do anything about the problem (by reporting it to those responsible). So, if confronted with faulty goods or services, for example, people are not very likely to actively complain.[21] Taking the motivation to moan to a new level might extend to, for example, letters voicing an objection about a particular issue sent to a newspaper and thereby shared with a wider audience. Of course, the leap from moaning to complaining is a tough one (Fox 2014). However, in connection to ADR, if people do access this service it can be perceived as giving voice to their complaint, making a stand, and having someone do something about it. This also enables the problem to be put right for future users.

The Justice System in Germany

In Germany, the court system is structured federally and its structure is divided between ordinary jurisdiction and specialized courts. The ordinary jurisdiction consists of the civil and criminal jurisdictions. The specialized courts are the administrative courts, the finance courts, the labour courts and the social courts. In addition, there is the constitutional jurisdiction, which consists of

[20] www.citizensadvice.org.uk.

[21] www.complaintexpert.co.uk/nation-complains-in-private.html.

the Federal Constitutional Court and the constitutional courts of the Länder. Further, the German court system is divided into five independent specialized branches of jurisdictions: ordinary jurisdiction, labour jurisdiction, general administrative jurisdiction, fiscal jurisdiction and social jurisdiction.[22]

A small claims procedure for claims under €600 is available in Germany. The court may, however, apply the ordinary procedure if the claim is too complex. Before going to court, parties must attempt in-court mediation. No appeal is possible, except in specific circumstances and 67.6% of the cases are dealt with within three months.[23] Consumer complaints are dealt with in an efficient way through the court system. The use of ADR is not widespread but, interestingly enough, in those sectors that have ADR bodies, they are mirroring the formal system (Creutzfeldt 2016e). What do I mean by that? The ADR landscape in Germany has developed slowly and was not particularly welcomed by the legal profession. Many lawyers thought that mediation and ADR would take away their business and allow 'amateurs' to take over. An observation about the ADR bodies in Germany (ombudsmen as a typical model) is that retired judges head them and employees are all trained lawyers. I will go into more detail about the significance of these characteristics in Chapter 6.

Verbraucherzentralen (Consumer Advice Centres)

All of the 16 *Länder* have *Verbraucherzentralen*—in total there are about 200 in Germany. The *Verbraucherzentralen* of the *Länder* and the central office combined have around 1000 employees. These facilities allow consumers to access reliable, up-to-date information and independent advice. The consumer centres are independent, mostly publicly funded, non-profit organizations. The aim of their work is to inform, advise and support consumers in private consumer matters. They offer help through disentangling the often complex market conditions and the resulting consumer confusion and complaints. Public funding is available to these consumer centres and they also generate some income through the sale of advice materials.

A Nation of Rules, Organization and Structure

Diverging briefly into stereotypes again. The Germans are said to have an extreme complaint culture. This is a result of the abundance of rules and laws that regulate many aspects of everyday life and the fact that people

[22] https://e-justice.europa.eu/content_judicial_systems_in_member_states-16-de-en.do?member=1.

[23] http://ec.europa.eu/consumers/solving_consumer_disputes/docs/ms_fiches_germany.pdf.

are used to obeying them. On the one hand, this leads to structure and efficiency and, on the other, to inflexibility. The love of rules manifests itself in many ways. For example, there is a very clear and authoritative language surrounding order.[24] In this culture there is little space for negotiating or allowing alternatives and a side effect of this is that consumers are not met with helpful or friendly customer services. A lot of complaints are therefore easily escalated to senior levels followed by legal action. One might argue that this forms part of the truth-seeking German mentality, being honest and outspoken without a defined sense of diplomacy or sensitivity. The notion is that complaining is often constructive, through seeking improvements, and German complainers are clear about what is bothering them.

Conclusion

In this chapter, I have explored European justice systems as a collection of national structures. A justice systems is understood here as the overarching framework of which a legal system is a part with its formal and informal pathways to redress. Our own national legal systems reflect how we behave and how we (as a country) expect people, organizations and governments to behave towards each other. Recent legislation on consumer ADR and ODR has introduced an EU-wide change to the informal dispute resolution landscape. The extent to which the informal ADR system is integrated alongside the formal legal system into the national justice system varies from country to country.

My aim in this book is to gain a better understanding of what people expect from their interactions with the informal ADR system when faced with problems and complaints about institutions. These complaints can be of civil and commercial nature (consumer to business) and of administrative justice nature (citizen and state). In this chapter I have argued that, for the legitimacy of the new legislative framework for ADR/ODR to be accepted, it needs to be understood in a national context and through its relationship with the formal legal system. The next chapter will discuss how ADR sits in the national justice systems and illustrate the differences and similarities between ombudsmen.

[24] I will return to this in Chapter 6 when disentangling the relationship people have with the justice system.

3

Models of Ombudsmen

Introduction

The tradition of settling disputes (Roberts and Palmer 2005) has its cultural origins in various nations around the world and there is no clear evidence or trace of where various models to resolve disputes originated. When discussing the ombudsman model of dispute resolution, the commonly portrayed origin is the Swedish model. The Swedish *Justitieombudsman*, established in 1809 (Anderman 1962), spread throughout other Nordic countries, to New Zealand in 1962, and then throughout the world (Reif 2004). The ombudsman institution filled a void in national legal systems offering a combination of redress and justice where there was a lack of respect for human rights. The ombudsman was imported to the national system to strengthen the existing legal order (Buck et al. 2011: 10). In other countries the ombudsman formed part of the expansion of the administrative sector (Heede 2000).

The ombudsman model was initially introduced as an administrative oversight and has since developed and grown beyond these tasks. The ombudsman model, part of a system to resolve people's complaints, is typically located within the national (social and political) context. Generally speaking, an ombudsman aims to restore public confidence in administration, in a sector, or in an individual institution or business. The ability of the ombudsman to operate comfortably in a range of different legal regimes, and perform the very different roles and functions that it has been used to deliver, is part of the success of the institution (Heede 2000; Kucsko-Stadlmayer 2009). A detailed historical overview of the ombudsman institution is provided

N. Creutzfeldt, *Ombudsmen and ADR*, Palgrave Socio-Legal Studies,
https://doi.org/10.1007/978-3-319-78807-4_3

Wby Reif (2004), setting out from its Swedish origins to its more modern incarnations, in the context of the human rights discourse. Seneviratne (2002) provides an overview of the public services ombudsmen in the administrative justice context and Buck et al. (2011) offer an account of the development of the ombudsman enterprise and administrative justice. I offer, in what follows, a brief overview of ombudsmen in the public sector, private sector and organizational ombudsmen (more detail Creutzfeldt 2018).

Types of Ombudsmen

A rather confusing thing about ombudsmen is that there are different types, providing different kinds of dispute resolution, yet they are all called ombudsmen. A broad distinction is that of public and private. But, if we were to question what exactly defines public and private (jurisdiction, funding, laws) we are likely to end up with a collection of hybrid structures with fuzzy boundaries. The following briefly outlines the similarities and differences between different types of ombudsmen.

The *public sector ombudsman* is set up by law to receive and investigate complaints from the public about state institutions. Some ombudsmen come with powers to investigate, others don't. A core role of a public sector ombudsman is to identify systemic problems as well as to investigate complaints. Ombudsmen typically look at lack of fairness on part of government administration (Reif 2004: 3). Ideally, they offer rapid and informal resolution to citizens' complaints and are seen as complementary, or supplementary, to the national court system (Rowat 2007).

The development of *private sector ADR* and, within this, the development of the ombudsman model, has become formalized in European legislation through the consumer alternative dispute resolution (ADR) directive (see Chapter 2) (Hodges et al. 2012). The ombudsman model is one of many forms an ADR body can have. For example, there are forms of ADR in the UK that are recognized by industries and run by the Institute of Dispute Resolution Schemes (IDRS) and the Chartered Institute of Arbitrators (CIArb). Then there are certified ADR bodies that have to be recognized as such by a competent authority. The competent authorities for regulated industries are usually the regulator of that sector. The legislation leaves it up to the member states to decide whether participation in ADR is mandatory for business. However the regulations do require most businesses that sell directly to consumers to signpost to a certified ADR body. A private sector ombudsman (or ADR provider) investigates consumers' complaints and aims to settle them.

The *organizational ombudsman* appeared spontaneously throughout the twentieth century (Rowe and Gadlin 2014). In the 1960s the classical ombudsman concept was adapted for organizations in many sectors. The organizational ombudsman offers a chance for people to raise issues and concerns in their lives as employees, managers, students, rather than as citizens. This model has evolved from the classic (public) ombudsman and can also be seen as a spontaneous creation and re-invention of an internal neutral conflict resolver (usually senior managers).

For the purpose of a general understanding of the ombudsman model I will discuss shared features and distinctive differences. The *shared* features are that ombudsmen offer an informal pathway to help people and business/institutions solve their grievances with each other. Usually ombudsmen are committed to a set of values that guide their standards, conduct and ethics. Compared to the formal system of dispute resolution (courts) the ombudsman model promises procedures that are speedy, cost-effective, and less formal. These promises are kept through a different process than that of a formal court procedure. Contact with an ombudsman typically does not take place face-to-face but over the phone, email or post. This is also how the information is shared, electronically.

The *differences* between public and private sector ombudsmen lie mainly in the type of problems they deal with. Public sector ombudsmen help citizens resolve problems with public institutions and private sector ombudsmen help consumers resolve problems with goods and services purchased from a business. A distinction can be found in the funding and the type of redress ombudsmen offer. Again, there are exceptions to the rule, but generally speaking public ombudsmen are funded though the public purse, whereas private ombudsmen are typically funded by their members' annual fees or sometimes through a combination of both.

For this study, clear distinctions are drawn between public ADR bodies and private ADR bodies. Private sector ADR bodies are those that fall under the consumer ADR directive and public sector ombudsmen are those set up by the government to help citizens bring problems they have with providers of public services (Table 3.1).

The consumer ADR directive creates challenges to ombudsmen in both private and public sectors. O'Brien (2015) argues that, 'in particular, those ombudsmen who currently oversee public bodies […] face the risk of relinquishing their distinctive democratic remit to a form of consumerism that is concerned exclusively with individual redress and market efficiency.' Might the ADR directive and its market driven outlook on consumerism influence the development of the public sector ombudsmen? O'Brien (2015) fears that the developments will distract from ombudsmen as ' … field-leaders in

Table 3.1 Public and private ombudsmen in this study

Country	Private sector ombudsmen	Public sector ombudsmen
Germany	Schlichtungsstelle für den öffentlichen Personenverkehr Schlichtungsstelle Energie Schlichtungsstelle Bundesnetzagentur Versicherungsombudsmann	
		Petitionsausschuss
United Kingdom	Legal Ombudsman Financial Ombudsman Services Ombudsman Services: Energy Ombudsman Services: Communications Ombudsman Services: Property	
		Parliamentary and Health Services Ombudsman Local Government Ombudsman

Table 3.2 Trust in justice

	Trust in the legal system [courts]	Trust in country's parliament	Trust in the police	Trust in the EP
UK	4.6	3.4	4.6	4.5
Germany	5.9	5.8	5.9	6.1

(Measured on a scale 1–10: 1 = no trust at all; 10 = complete trust)

the era of new governance and of the pragmatic turn in the construction of legal liberalism.' Maintaining a clear divide between public and private then, the future of public sector ombudsmen is 'a matter of democratic accountability rather than of consumer redress.'

I don't share O'Brien's fear; rather I believe that there is an opportunity for the public sector ombudsmen to benefit from the current debate about quality of service and user satisfaction that is dominating the debate around the private sector ombudsmen, and ADR as a whole (Creutzfeldt and Bradford 2018). Equally, the public sector ombudsmen can develop and foster their role of holding government bodies to account as well as to engage with citizens' expectations and grievances. I will return to this discussion in Chapter 8.

Harmonization vs Diversity of Setting

The aim of the European Union (EU) consumer ADR and online dispute resolution (ODR) legislation is to provide a harmonized approach to consumer redress throughout the EU. As discussed in Chapter 2, EU member states have different legal traditions, different legal systems and different legal cultures. The consumer ADR directive offered member states a framework to adapt into their national specific contexts.

The ambitions of the EU are straightforward; this legislation was born out of the need to encourage consumption in the single market and to set up institutions that provide redress in case of problems. These institutions are required to be cheap, accessible and fair and are intended to provide speedy resolution (Creutzfeldt 2016b). Like most pieces of harmonized legislation, having gone through a process of community scrutiny, the ADR directive was a compromise. The legislation had to fit in with existing ADR bodies in the member states and, on top of that, provide (minimum) guidelines and quality criteria for the creation of new ones. Many commentators believe that these guidelines are not strict enough and leave too much leeway in the interpretation of the directive into national systems (Kirkham 2016; Creutzfeldt and Berlin 2016; Gill et al. 2017).

Implementation into the national legal space continues to be challenging. Every member state has its own traditions and legal systems that have contributed towards their approaches to disputes, attitudes to institutions and that influence what citizens expect of those institutions. To be successfully integrated into the national setting we need to consider more than just the rules and anticipated institutional requirements of ombudsmen. Although the consumer ADR directive covers disputes between consumers and businesses, it has forced member states to engage in a wider debate about the provision of ADR in general. ADR cannot be seen as a standalone process, it needs to be viewed within the environment in which it is supposed to function and must take into account the people it is designed to serve. This includes the public sector ombudsmen as well. It is a system of informal justice that is closely intertwined with the formal justice system (see Chapter 2).

The Development of the Ombudsman Model in the National Context

Some noteworthy post-World War II political developments contributed to the necessity of establishing an independent office that would be responsible for reinstating confidence on legal continuity, redress and justice, and that would operate according to the principles of fairness and equity. This resulted in a multitude of different ombudsmen, situated in different contexts. Therefore, ombudsmen need to be understood not only in the context of the overall purpose they serve but also where they are situated within their national context.[1] A common theme within the diversity of contexts into which the ombudsmen has been transplanted is a response, reaction or sought-for solution for filling an identified gap. This gap could be either a lack of public accountability and need for an intermediary between the citizen and the state in the public sector; or the identified lack of access to justice for resolving consumer complaints in the private sector, for example. Of course, the drivers for change that prompted the development and spread of the ombudsman model have different backgrounds and with the proliferation of the model the diversity of processes and decision-making also developed (Creutzfeldt 2018).

As mentioned, the ombudsman model I am concerned with was created in Sweden to give the people a voice to place complaints against the monarch (Creutzfeldt 2018). It developed into a model to improve citizens' rights and their ability to enforce accountability in the political and administrative process. The Swedish ombudsman model grew and expanded over the centuries within the context of the national legal culture (Reif 2013). This, arguably, produced a national socialization and acceptance of this model. From there it travelled to other places. But what does this transplantation mean for the acceptance of a new model into a system that has no concrete experience of or socialization towards ombudsmen or ADR?

Relocated into new settings the ombudsman model requires a flexible approach to the context in which it will resolve disputes. This shift and development of the model has happened alongside the changing relationship between the individual and the state. The relationships are constantly redefined as part of our interactions with public service providers or businesses from which we purchase goods and services. These everyday encounters are subject to two overarching relationships, that between the citizen and the state and that between the consumer and the business. These are subject to constant negotiation, based on people's overarching attitudes to, and expectations of, authorities.

These two sets of pertinent relationships—citizen/state and consumer/business—have, of course, many interwoven dimensions and are informed by different channels. The relationship between the citizen and the state is informed through a combination of long and short-term political changes, socio-economic developments and our immediate personal surroundings, to name a few. From this vast mix of information and realities that we are faced with, fuelled constantly by the media and the internet, we have to choose a version or position from which to negotiate our environment.

---

[1] This, I suggest, has an effect on their acceptance by their users (Creutzfeldt 2016d).

Our opinions are shaped and reshaped by the manner in which we collect information about daily encounters with the state, the legal system and its institutions of authority. I suggest that the way in which we learn to accept, criticize and question these official institutions—either through direct interaction or through other channels—governs our assumptions and expectations of our relationships with other institutions in a system. Put differently, we will use what we believe to be true about authority as a blueprint to shape our attitudes towards another form of authority in the justice system.

The relationship between the consumer and a business is constantly being modified and renegotiated. There are many reasons for this, for example, the opening of the marketplace to competition, or the opportunity to compare goods and services online and purchase across national borders. As consumers today, we have a choice to actively engage with the business we purchase a good or service from. We can compare offers, change suppliers and complain when things go wrong. Consumers' demands for fair treatment, being more aware of their rights, and the availability of digital technology have all contributed to generating an informed and educated consumer.[2] Consumers demand better services and this includes a well-functioning dispute resolution provision.

The way in which citizens relate to institutions providing public services (Creutzfeldt 2016d) and the way in which consumers relate to a business will be at their most fragile when bringing a complaint. What both situations have in common is that the individual is usually in the weaker position in a dispute with a public body or a business. Here the ombudsman comes into play. It operates at the intersection between the relationships and negotiates them. Based on our relationship with authority, we make sense of this interaction. The authorities that shape our expectations are part of our legal and political culture (Hertogh and Kurkchiyan 2016).

How then can we best understand the development of the ombudsman model in its national setting? As the model was taken from its Swedish origins into other cultural contexts, the literature on legal transplants and legal culture seems the most promising approach by which to understand this process.

In this chapter, I continue to build the argument that ombudsmen can only be accepted and trusted as part of a justice system when understood in their national context. To grasp the tension between informal flexibility

[2] *The Guardian* 'The relationship between consumers and business is changing from the bottom up' 26 January 2012: https://www.theguardian.com/sustainable-business/davos-consumer-business-relationship.

and context, the first part lays the foundations for this discussion, drawing upon the literature on legal transplants and legal culture. In this setting, the ombudsman—as an ADR model prescribed by European legislators to be made available—is evaluated as a legal transplant, operating in a specific legal culture. The overarching question here is whether the ombudsman model is replicable in every local cultural context. To explore this idea, the second part of the chapter goes on to apply these concepts of transplants and legal culture as a window onto the case studies.

Transplanting the Ombudsman Model into the National Legal Space

Comparative law scholars have described legal transplants as either a theory of legal change, or as a shared technique used by political agents to borrow rules, institutions, or principles from other places. This makes a transplant more of a technique, rather than generating legal change. Watson (1974: 21), coining the term, described legal transplants as 'the moving of a rule or a system of law from one country to another or from one people to another'. According to Watson's theory, a legal rule is transplanted simply because it is a good idea. He further states that 'transplanting is, in fact, the most fertile source of development. Most changes in most systems are the result of borrowing' (Watson 1993: 93).

In a critique of Watson's (1993) claim that the transplantation of legal rules 'travel[s] across jurisdictions, which are displaced, which are transplanted', Legrand (1997) argues that interactions across legal systems need to be understood in their complex set of historical, epistemological, or cultural contexts that shape a law and rules. Because rules are not socially connected in any meaningful way, differences in 'historical factors and habits though do not limit or qualify their transplantablility' (p. 113). Legrand (1997) disagrees with Watson's understanding of rules and argues that rules cannot travel and therefore legal transplants are impossible (1993: 114). Carrying the argument for an inclusion of surrounding factors of a potential transplant (Mauss 1995: 274–275) argues that 'every manifestation of the law – a rule, for instance – must be apprehended a complete social fact'. Building on the notion that law cannot be understood in isolation from its surroundings (Roscoe 1938: 94) explores the idea that the 'history of a system of law is largely a history of borrowings of legal materials from other legal systems and of assimilation of materials from outside of the law.'

The choice of interpretations of any given system of law and what are the side-effects of its transplantation into another system could be assessed from countless angles. Indeed, it is not possible to understand a transplanted institution or system in isolation, rather it needs to evolve into its surroundings. Equally, the surroundings will have an influence on the transplant. Therefore, I have some sympathy with Legrand's view that rules are connected to a set of cultural meanings and understandings and that the latter do not move with the rules. Rather rules, when travelling with the legal transplant, are given new meanings according to their context. This, I believe, is the strength of the ombudsman model—it is not a set rule or law that is imposed into a new system, rather it is an idea or model that can be adapted into new contexts and therefore, potentially, create its own culture and specific rules. I take the view that understanding the law can only be achieved if the law is manifested and accepted through rules that cannot be disentangled from their cultural, historical and ideological constructions. It is also the case that context and local meaning matter. Therefore, I argue that an ombudsman model understood not as an imposed or transplanted set of rules but rather as a flexible model that comes with a set of tools designed to fit into an existing legal system has proven to be a successful approach. This model, if we stick with the notion of legal transplant, could be understood as a borrowed model that has been introduced to a new surrounding and has to evolve into becoming part of it. The question remains though of how the ombudsman model is accepted within its new setting which, I believe, happens through the lens of people's culturally determined understandings of a legal system[3] (Chapter 6). Consequently, in the ombudsman context, it is not so much the question of whether a set of rules can or cannot be transplanted from one culture to another, but rather how this model can be adjusted to suit the system into which it has been integrated. This means that any given national legal culture and legal system into which the ombudsman has been introduced plays a part in how the model is accepted by its users.

What then makes us accept an ombudsman? Part of the answer to this question lies in the role of national legal culture and the cultures of legality of which we are part.

[3]Of course policy makers and the legislature will have also influenced the adaptation of the ombudsman model. The Police Complaints Authority for instance drew on the Scandinavian model but was very much a product of the UK's particular political and constitutional system in the 1950 and 1960s.

The Role of Legal Culture and Cultures of Legality

The next layer in this discourse is the question of how much our disputing behaviour and settlement seeking is a product of our (legal) culture? What motivates people to use an ombudsman system and what shapes their attitudes towards it? One possible explanation is that legal culture produces a specific national approach of disputing and settlement. The concept of legal culture has been written about at length from national and comparative perspectives (Nelken 2004; Friedman 1969). Legal culture is a widely debated and contested concept. I am not proposing here to engage in the debate of how best to understand it. What I will offer, however, is a brief discussion and thereby a lens though which the country case studies can be seen to assist the understanding of how the institution of an ombudsman sits within a national system.

In an attempt to deconstruct the rather complex notion of legal culture (Merry 1987) starts by choosing a specific perspective through which to approach the concept. She proposes three options: comparative law (legal families and traditions, examining how they develop and how they cluster together), anthropology (the way law expresses ideas and values that are shared with the larger society, both reflecting and creating these larger systems of thought and action); and a socio-legal perspective (law in context—the way in which institutions operate in everyday practice). The present discussion approaches the idea from the socio-legal perspective and I start with (Friedman 1969) who championed the law-in-action movement. He was convinced that formal law in the books received too much weight and instead proposed that law in action should receive more attention. Within this endeavour, Friedman described a divide which was evident when studying legal culture empirically: the option of an analytical concept within a more established theory of social relations, or as a measurable concrete term. The analytical framework understands legal culture to include patterns of citizen behaviour with respect to the legal system, their judgements about laws, fairness, legitimacy and utility. These patterns and attitudes vary according to state or group and form the legal culture of organizations, groups, or a state (Friedman 1969; Silbey 2010). Along similar lines Cotterrell (1998: 31–32) argues that legal culture 'determines and is determined by perceptions and expectations of law and justice: how authority and procedure should be organized and how to judge whether it is legitimate and effective, and decides whether in concrete cases justice has been done.'

Finally, there is Nelken's (2004: 1) definition of legal culture: 'legal culture in its most general sense is one way of describing relatively stable patterns of legally oriented social behaviour and attitudes'. Thus, any given legal culture consists of a combination of its institutions, ideas, attitudes and values.

Moving from the broad understanding of legal culture to a more situated, contextualized analysis of sites of social action, the *cultural turn* in socio-legal studies (Silbey 2010) allowed the researcher to focus more on everyday encounters and interactions with legal systems.

> The turn to everyday life and the cultural meanings of social action demanded a willingness to shift from naïve categories of actors as the object of study to an analytically conceptualized unit of analysis, the researcher's definition of the subject: legal culture. Legality is an ongoing structure of social action. (Ewick and Silbey 1998: 55–56)

I am interested in exploring public knowledge of and attitudes towards justice systems; system that, similar to the concept of culture, have no clear boundaries. How then is legality constructed? The idea of law in combination with a popularly shared understanding of what law is and how it matters in everyday life are the building blocks of legality. Legal cultures can be understood as representative structures of legality. This means that legal culture can be explored through its institutions as well as through the people that interact with the system. To achieve this, I propose to look at how institutions of the informal justice system construct legality and how people's legal consciousness (and legal socialization) plays a crucial role in its acceptance. The following section will therefore introduce Blankenburg's understanding of legal culture as provided by legal infrastructure. The empirical data collected for this project will pick up on the interaction of supply (ombudsman) and demand (people) in Chapter 6.

Returning to the complexity of the concept of legal culture and defining its boundaries, the national level is chosen here as a unit of analysis. Nelken (2013) argues that the national level is a good starting point. Equally, Hofstede (2001) argues for an understanding of national culture as 'a collective programming of the mind'. This manifests itself in values, symbols, rituals and institutions that become more influential when they have been legitimized by cultural norms. Within the unit of national boundaries and treating an ombudsman model as part of a legal system's infrastructure, do patterns of legal cultures and theory of legal infrastructure help explain people's use of ombudsmen in a legal system? Might they even create their own category in a culture of legality? This collective construction of legality—that is 'forms of consciousness combine to constitute ideological or hegemonic legality'—will be empirically studied in Chapter 6.

The Notion of Legal Culture as Legal Infrastructure

Returning to the question of the influence of legal culture on disputing behaviour, Blankenburg offers an interesting argument. He suggests that legal cultures can be measured through legal behaviour, encouraged by the availability of institutions (and amount of legal professionals).

Blankenburg compared the Netherlands and Germany and measured the two countries' legal cultures through indicators (institutions) such as legal education, the legal profession, civil and criminal justice, and the institutions of administrative and constitutional review. He found that, despite Germany and the Netherlands having strong cultural and legal communalities (legal traditions, political histories and legal histories), when comparing institutions and legal behaviour there are clear differences (i.e. frequency of litigation and number of lawyers).

> German legal culture offers less of an avoidance infrastructure than that of the Netherlands ... legal behaviour is determined by institutional supply rather than by popular demand (the Netherlands has many alternatives to litigation). (Blankenburg 1997: 20)

Blankenburg claims that 'folk culture' shapes differences in legal behaviour (related to the stereotypes introduced in Chapter 2); the institutional and infrastructure arrangements represent the key to differences in legal culture (civil litigation rates being indicators of legal culture). This means that there are differences in the functioning of the law (in an everyday setting), thus resulting in communalities of legal systems.[4] Why? According to Blankenburg it is because the regulations that produce differences in legal behaviour are hidden and detailed in the institutional infrastructure. Blankenburg concludes by stating that similarities of formal legal systems are bad predictors of how legal cultures actually work.

How do legal cultures work? Applying Blankenburg's approach of 'supply and demand' of legal infrastructure to the ombudsman model: if countries had comparable ADR schemes would they be used in the same way? As mentioned above, in the private ombudsman context, there are EU-wide requirements to have ADR providers in every member state with shared, regulated quality criteria. In Blankenburg's terms, the institutional infrastructure (supply) is now (mostly) available. However, the demand has

[4] Elements of the puzzle of comparative legal culture include: the legal profession; access to justice; courts and litigation; civil litigation; criminal courts; special tribunals; and the concept of legal culture.

not caught up. What we can see from the existing ADR landscape in the EU is that ADR is used and accepted very differently. What can be extracted from these considerations is the question of whether institutional culture is more important in the ombudsman or ADR context than legal culture. I believe it is important to take into account these two concepts in understanding the development of the ombudsman model. However, these concepts are only theoretically separate from each other—in reality they are closely interwoven. Blankenburg argues that the available infrastructure for dispute resolution—in our example, the availability of ADR—produces disputing behaviour, producing legal culture. What about the people who use the system (demand side)? I believe that the people who use the ombudsman have a part to play in the development of disputing behaviour and acceptance of those institutions. We bring our understanding and expectations of processes with us, influenced by previous experiences and other forms of socialization. Therefore, I suggest extending Blankenburg's thesis of focusing on the *supply side* of providing a legal (institutional) culture to inquiring further into the *demand side*. Here, I would like to depart from Blankenburg's terminology which infers an economic appreciation of the dynamic between people and institutions. My preferred way of exploring this dynamic and its human side is to reflect upon people's relationships with and understandings of the law. So I suggest that, rather than labelling it *demand side*, the lens of legal consciousness and legal socialization should be applied for a richer appreciation of how people who use the available legal infrastructure make sense of these institutions and their authority.

Legal Culture as Infrastructure and Consciousness

Understanding legal culture as a mixture of its institutional infrastructure and people's consciousness allows for a more fine grained and rounded inquiry. The notion of culture as producing patterns of legality that orient social behaviour and attitudes (Nelken 2004) can be explored in a more nuanced way though people's interactions with institutions of the justice system. Following on from the importance of appreciating the human quality of legal culture, the intellectual lineage between legal culture, law as culture and legal consciousness need to be examined. I posit here that what (Rosen 2008), an anthropologist, has described as *law as culture* can be translated into the way in which the relationships between individuals form vis-à-vis the institutions making decisions and handing down decisions. Rosen describes law as culture as:

> … the facts that are adduced in a legal forum connect to the ways in which facts are constructed in other areas of everyday life, how the processes of legal decision-making partake of the logic by which the culture as a whole is put together, and how courts, mediators, or social pressures fashion a sense of the world as consistent with common sense and social identity. (Rosen 2008: 8)

I believe that this describes what happens when we interact with legal institutions and how we use these experiences to make sense of our relationship with authorities. Put differently, legal culture is so much more than its legal institutions. This idea is expressed in similar ways throughout the literature, taking on different forms and focus. Legal culture encompasses the effect its institutions have on individuals who are part of the overall system, as well as how these individuals make sense of that system. This boils down to people's relationship with the law being shaped by their experiences with and expectations of the institutions and authorities they encounter. Socialization, as I argue later in this book, forms a blueprint of expectations towards institutions of the justice system. The progression of this proposition would be to argue that the institutions within a legal culture produce their own sense of legality that then influences how other institutions are viewed. This prospect will be empirically explored in Chapters 5 and 6.

Country Case Studies: Negotiating Relationships with Authority

What becomes apparent from the discussion above on transplanting dispute resolution models and thinking about legal infrastructure is that we are looking at different sets of relationships that are constantly being negotiated and revisited and that even influence each other. These relationships are those between the citizen and the state (public sector ombudsmen) and between the consumer and the business (private sector ombudsmen). The overarching relationship is the one that citizens develop, and constantly negotiate, with authorities. This then begs closer examination of the national infrastructure into which ADR is being introduced. Guiding questions here are:

- Is the ombudsman model replicable?
- Does it have the same kind of meaning in different national contexts?

Things to acknowledge at this stage are twofold. First, there is no literature to my knowledge that has looked at ombudsmen in a cross-national comparison or examined them through the lens of the justice system and their place therein. I therefore rely on my data to propose some explanation of how I understand the development of ADR occurs in the national context. Second, although I appreciate that there are many dimensions to the relationships people form with authorities and with the state, for the purpose of my deliberations I shall focus on the most prominent relationships which, I believe, assist our understanding of how the ombudsman finds its place within a given system of justice. This, in turn, influences the way in which it is accepted and trusted (or not) by its users. In other words, although no national level is cohesive in its justice systems, there is a national order that is valuable as a reference point in the study of ombudsmen.

The following section will look at the country case studies with a focus on uncovering some of the nationally and culturally distinct features of each legal system. The intention is to understand not only how the ombudsmen operate in different country settings, but also how the institutional and political environment matters and contributes to people making sense of the legal system and of ombudsmen.

Supporting the argument that I develop in this chapter, I will briefly present some European Social Survey (ESS) statistics relating to the trust people express towards the (formal) justice systems.[5] This data, I suggest, provides an avenue into understanding how people form their expectations of the informal system. Both the formal and informal justice systems offer pathways to justice. This means that together they provide an overarching system for dispute resolution and thus will have some influence upon each other. This influence, I suggest, is specific to each country's system and will be discussed in more detail in Chapter 6. Studies about pathways to formal justice have found that attitudes towards the courts influence people's propensity to use them (Genn and Beinart 1999: 228). Is this finding transferable to the ADR context? As I will establish in my empirical chapter (Chapter 4), the perceived trust and legitimacy of an ombudsman has an impact on decision-acceptance. This might contribute, amongst other factors, to trust and a propensity to use ADR.

The results of Round 5—'trust in justice'—of the ESS[6] form the beginning of my argument; that trust and attitudes associated with the formal legal system shape or influence our attitudes and expectations towards the developing informal system. It is, of course, not quite as straightforward a relationship as that. As the book unfolds, the various nuances and influ-

[5] www.europeansocialsurvey.org/about/.

[6] *Trust in Justice*: round 5: www.europeansocialsurvey.org/docs/findings/ESS5_toplines_issue_1_trust_in_justice.pdf.

ences will be explored theoretically (Chapter 3) and empirically (Chapters 5 and 6) to then be brought together in Chapters 4 and 5 (Table 3.2).

Because ADR has been required by European legislators to be a part of the national informal justice architecture though the consumer ADR directive, we now have the opportunity to begin to monitor this process of acceptance. The present study provides the first set of comparable empirical evidence to be able to start to understand the role that ADR plays in the national justice system. It is important to mention here the debate on the relationship between the formal justice system and ADR as it feeds into the national acceptance of informal systems. The procedures and outcomes that courts and ADR can provide are different.

Courts and ADR Bodies: Formal Decisions vs Informal Resolution

The role of (evolving and established) ADR schemes in national settings in Europe has led to some confusion about their relationship to the court system.[7] The main concern is that ADR potentially doubles the avenues for consumer redress and thereby weakens the courts' jurisdiction in consumer matters. The debate therefore focuses on the relationship between existing and developing ADR pathways and the courts: will ADR compete with the courts? Does ADR bring any added value to a legal system? How can a high level of procedural quality be established when ADR is aimed at being faster and more cost-efficient than courts?

The lack of empirical evidence on European ADR models makes it currently impossible to answer these questions. However, it is possible to identify the main focus of the current debate. Three central themes emerge:

1. types of disputes;
2. objectives and criteria; and
3. significance of litigation for an ADR approach.

First, the *types of disputes* that are brought to an ADR body are low-value claims that would not typically be brought to a court. Consumers who bring complaints to court typically claim that the process is too costly,

[7]This notion of concern was very apparent at the first ADR conference 'Schlichten statt Klagen: Alternative Formen der Streitbeilegung', in Germany in November 2012; available at: http://www.bmelv.de/SharedDocs/Standardartikel/Verbraucherschutz/Markt-Recht/SchlichtenStattKlagen.html.

time-consuming and not user-friendly. ADR schemes are designed to resolve complaints (ideally) at no cost to the consumer and in a fast, efficient, user-friendly and effective manner.[8]

Second, assessment *objectives and criteria* differ between the *interest-based* ADR procedure and the *legally based* court procedure. This means that a court procedure and an ADR procedure have different objectives. While a court process is aimed at enforcing legal positions and thereby might exacerbate the conflict, ADR (at least those procedures without a binding decision, like mediation and conciliation) is aimed at reaching a satisfactory outcome for both sides involved. The ADR procedure and court procedure criteria differ in that the former does not require stringent application of established legal principles.

Matters of the law are traditionally not of primary concern in the ADR procedure. Although most European ADR schemes are expected to follow the principle of legality and review the law in relation to weighting the interests of the parties as stated in 98/257/EG,[9] the application thereof is inconsistent (Alleweldt 2011). The most recent version of the ADR directive, however, makes the principle of legality mandatory in Article 11.[10] Of course, one can argue that the law is not the only reference when finding a solution in an ADR procedure. Rather, it can be seen as a standard to enable the parties to evaluate their positions and provide the option of an informed decision for the evaluation of the ADR process (Alexander et al. 2005). To clarify, the ADR approach consists of an initial rights-based approach to determine the remit, followed by a stage of a comprehensive interest-based approach.

The third theme is the *importance of litigation for the ADR approach.* Most ADR procedures are based on voluntary participation by companies.[11] At any point in the ADR process, there is the option to take the complaint to court, complying with constitutional requirements that the pathway to the courts has to remain open to resolve a dispute. In some cases, if there is no existing

---

[8]The public consultation on the use of ADR as a means to resolve disputes related to commercial transactions and practices in the EU summary of the responses received 2011; available at: http://ec.europa.eu/consumers/redress_cons/Feedback_Statement_Final.pdf.

[9]98/257/EC Commission Recommendation of 30 March 1998 on the principles applicable to the bodies responsible for out-of-court settlement of consumer disputes; available at: http://eur-lex.europa.eu/LexUriServ/LexUriServ.do?uri=OJ:L:1998:115:0031:0034:EN:PDF.

[10]Directive 2013/11/EU of the European Parliament and of the Council on Alternative Dispute Resolution for Consumer Disputes and Amending Regulation (EC) No 2006/2004 and Directive 2009/22/EC (directive on consumer ADR): http://eur-lex.europa.eu/LexUriServ/LexUriServ.do?uri=OJ:L:2013:165:0063:0079:EN:PDF.

[11]The exceptions are the telecom and energy sectors, where joining an ADR scheme is mandatory.

case law, an ADR scheme can refer the case to the courts; this is normally specified in the ADR scheme's procedural rules and in the most recent ADR directive. On the other hand, courts value the work of ombudsmen and their decisions, as documented for public sector ombudsmen (Kirkham 2005: 387).

The procedural rules of ombudsmen are more flexible, take a shorter time than a court process and have a very low cost risk for the consumer. The ombudsman procedure is designed to be more accessible than a court and there is no need for legal representation. Aiming at an agreement through a facilitated process that is understandable forms 'part of social elements that may complement the civil suit rooted in the rule of law … ADR corresponds with a modern understanding of consumer protection and demonstrates that companies meet their social responsibility' (Hirsch 2013: 2).

The expansion and implementation of ADR into the justice system follows the logic that certain types of complaints are better suited for an informal procedure, as compared to a formal route. ADR is expected to fill a well-documented gap in access to justice for consumers in Europe by providing accessible, fast, affordable and independent redress. This affects each jurisdiction in a different way. One aspect of this is how we, as the users of these systems, make sense of this comparatively new system of redress.

German Case Study

Since the implementation of the consumer ADR directive into national law in 2016, Germany made available private sector ADR bodies for most sectors and, for those areas producing consumer detriment that are not covered, a residual body has been created in Kehl.[12] It is difficult to assess how many ADR bodies there currently are in Germany as the numbers are changing. One indication is the number registered with the European Commission (EC). Member states are obliged to notify the number of ADR providers operating in their country that are meeting the standards set out by the ADR directive. Germany has notified 22 ADR bodies to the EC.[13] These bodies are mainly for banks, insurance, transport, energy and telecoms in the private sector. The types of ADR practised are arbitration, conciliation and mediation procedures. These are used to supplement each other, but each procedure is distinct.[14]

[12]https://www.verbraucher-schlichter.de/herzlich-willkommen-bei-der-allgemeinen-verbraucherschlichtungsstelle-—ihrer-schlichtungsstelle-fuer-verbraucherstreitigkeiten.

[13]https://webgate.ec.europa.eu/odr/main/index.cfm?event=main.adr.show.

[14]http://ec.europa.eu/civiljustice/adr/adr_ger_en.htm.

Germany, due to its historical and political development, has no public sector ombudsman that can be compared to other countries. The closest to a body that provides an avenue for citizens to voice concerns about state bodies is the *Petitionsausschuss*. Also called 'Parliament's seismograph',[15] it has a mandate to examine the impact of legislation on the population (Deutscher Bundestag 2015). Individuals send letters with requests or complaints addressed to the Bundestag (the lower house of the German Parliament). These are then passed on to the Committee, which examines and deliberates on these petitions. This makes it a 'seismograph' which records the mood among the population, on the basis that citizens are best placed to say whether legislation: is achieving its intended aims; or causing new problems and, therefore, needs to be reviewed critically; or that the Bundestag should take action to address a particular concern. The *Petitionsausschuss* was part of my study but, unfortunately, only 24 individuals responded to the survey. This is not enough data to make valid comparable quantitative claims. It will, however, inform the qualitative analysis in Chapter 6.

As set out in Chapter 2, the German legal system is known to be efficient, accessible and able to deal with complaints in a timely manner. Related to the expectations of efficiency, the ADR bodies in Germany are set up in the same manner as the courts, with a (retired) judge at the top as ombudsman and legal staff under her or him. This produces the air of a formal process and the national implementation of the ADR directive ensures that the legalistic context and setting is maintained. This gives the informal dispute resolution model a very formal character.

This formality is reflected in the ADR bodies that have been part of this study (Creutzfeldt 2016c): that is, four private sector ADR bodies covering transport, energy, telecoms and financial services: The *Schlichtungsstelle für den öffentlichen Personenverkehr* was founded in December 2009 and deals with complaints about travel by train, bus, aeroplane and ship. For the present study, only airline disputes are considered. These are dealt with online and are mainly about delays, cancellations and baggage.[16] The *Schlichtungsstelle Energie* is the conciliation body for energy and is an independent and neutral institution that deals with disputes between energy companies and their consumers. The *Schlichtungsstelle Energie* is jointly funded by the Verbraucherzentrale Bundesverband eV. and the associations of the energy market.[17] The *Schlichtungsstelle Telekommunikation* is

[15]http://www.bundestag.de/htdocs_e/bundestag/committees/a02.

[16]Söp Report (2015) from my project: https://www.law.ox.ac.uk/sites/files/oxlaw/oxford_bericht_teil_soep.pdf.

[17]Schlichtungsstelle Energie Report (2015) from my project: https://www.law.ox.ac.uk/sites/files/oxlaw/schlieenergie_bericht.pdf.

the conciliation body for telecommunications and aims to settle disputes between providers of telecommunication services and their customers. The conciliation body has been running since 1999 as a neutral body, created by the Telekommunikationsgesetz (the law for telecommunications). In April 2016, the *Schlichtungsstelle Telekommunikation* was renamed *Schlichtungsstelle Bundesnetzagentur*. The Bundesnetzagentur is the regulator for telecoms in Germany. The *Versicherungsombudsmann* (insurance ombudsman) was founded in 2001. German insurance providers founded the ombudsman to help protect consumers and to prevent a court case when a dispute arises.[18]

The lack of an ADR tradition in Germany, I hypothesize, manifests itself in a lack of trust in the concept of ADR. Therefore, for users in Germany to accept an ombudsman model, a mirror image of the formal justice system is created. Through this, the relationship towards authority is taken into account and an ADR procedure has been put in place that is very similar to a formal procedure. As will be seen in the empirical Chapters 5 and 6, this formality is reflected in the institutional set-up of the ombudsmen and the outcomes they recommend.

UK Case Study

The UK has a large ADR and ombudsman landscape, offering a variety of different models and procedures for consumers to seek redress (Creutzfeldt 2016a; Kirkham 2016). However, there are currently no ombudsmen schemes for many areas of consumer goods and services (Gill et al. 2017). The UK also has several ombudsmen that address public sector grievances. Ombudsmen services attract thousands of claims per year and in the UK and Ireland there are 26 ombudsmen across public and private sectors (Ombudsman Association UK members).[19] The respective workloads vary and they deal with different types of complaints. As has been argued elsewhere, an individual who approaches an ombudsman with a private sector complaint (e.g. telecoms or furniture) is less likely to have a deep emotional engagement with the issues concerned as a person who approaches a public sector ombudsman about a health or government-related issue.

[18]Versicherungsombudsmann Report (2015) from my project: https://www.law.ox.ac.uk/sites/files/oxlaw/oxford_bericht_teil_vo.pdf.

[19]The Ombudsman Association: http://www.ombudsmanassociation.org. For a list as of 2017, see page 10 of the 2017 Annual Report: http://www.ombudsmanassociation.org/docs/Annual_report_OA_16-17_Final.pdf. That total of 31 ombudsman members does not only include ombudsman in the UK, but also in Ireland, the British Crown Dependencies and the British Overseas Territories.

Complaints brought to a public sector ombudsman are usually complex and involve a cluster of entangled issues. Additionally, taxpayers finance the public ombudsmen and this cultivates a sense of entitlement in relation to the service provided. In contrast, the private sector ombudsmen are typically funded by the industry they serve. This, in turn, can have an effect on perceived independence. The number of UK ADR providers notified to the EC is 43,[20] so the coverage is broader compared to that of Germany, with ADR bodies offering redress for a larger variety of sectors. The different types of ADR practised in England and Wales—listed on the European Judicial Network site of the EC—are ombudsmen, regulators, arbitration, mediation, neutral evaluation, conciliation, expert determination, neutral fact-finding, and mediation and arbitration (medarb).[21]

One noticeable difference between the two countries in this study is that the UK has a few umbrella ADR providers, meaning that one body offers ADR for different sectors.[22] Although this seems to be a good way to enhance visibility for the consumer, the ADR landscape remains difficult to understand, especially since the UK has a variety of ADR bodies that are embedded in the national justice system. The challenge for the consumer is to find the right body for their complaint (Gill et al. 2017). The ADR landscape therefore remains very difficult to navigate, with ADR bodies competing for consumers (Gill et al. 2017).

The national court system is known to be difficult to access and is unpredictable in terms of outcomes, costs and duration of cases. It has been said that 'justice in the UK is open to all, like the Ritz hotel' (Bingham 2011: 86). Usually, consumers would not try to bring their complaints to court as it involves fees, uncertainty, and more often than not the value of the claim is not high enough to make it worthwhile. I would suggest that the fairly low expectations of the national court system in the UK reflect the population's attitude to expectations and acceptance of authorities. This is why ADR has developed in a less formal manner. Compared to the German system, it is minimally legalistic and prides itself on simple processes and accessibility.

The UK ADR bodies that have been part of this study are two public sector ombudsmen and five private sector ombudsmen (Creutzfeldt 2015, 2016c).

[20]https://webgate.ec.europa.eu/odr/main/index.cfm?event=main.adr.show.

[21]http://ec.europa.eu/civiljustice/adr/adr_uni_en.htm.

[22]For example, Ombudsman Services offers ADR for telecoms, energy, property and consumers.

The *Parliamentary and Health Services Ombudsman* (PHSO) is one of the two public sector bodies in the study. The PHSO makes final decisions on complaints that have not been resolved by the National Health Service in England, UK government departments or other UK public organizations. The other public sector ombudsman is the *Local Government Ombudsman* (LGO). The LGO looks at complaints about councils and some other authorities and organizations, including education admissions appeal panels and adult social care providers (such as care homes and home care providers).

The *Legal Ombudsman* (LeO) was established by the Legal Services Act 2007 and approved by the Legal Services Board and the Lord Chancellor. The LeO is a scheme set up to help resolve different types of legal service disputes. It can look into complaints about all sorts of regulated legal service providers: solicitors; barristers; licensed conveyancers; cost lawyers; legal executives; notaries; patent attorneys; trade mark attorneys; law firms; and companies providing legal services such as claims management companies.

The *Financial Ombudsman Service* (FOS) is the largest ombudsman in Europe. The FOS looks at complaints about most financial problems involving: payment protection insurance; banking; insurance; mortgages; credit cards and store cards; loans and credit; payday lending and debt collecting; pensions; savings and investments; hire purchase and pawnbroking; money transfer; financial advice; stocks; shares; unit trusts; and bonds.

Ombudsman Services is an umbrella ombudsman that provides dispute resolution for several sectors. The following three were part of this study. *Ombudsman Services: Energy* deals with: problems with energy bills; problems resulting from an energy company's sales activity; problems resulting from switching gas or electricity supplier; physical problems relating to the supply of energy to a home or small business, such as power cuts and connections; micro-generation and feed-in tariffs; and problems relating to the provision of services under the Green Deal.[23] *Ombudsman Services: Communications* looks at: billing problems; problems resulting from a company's sales activity; problems resulting from switching from one company to another; poor service, for example, failing to act on a request; premium rate services; pay TV; voice-on demand; and mobile phone handsets. Finally, *Ombudsman Services: Property* deals with: apparent breaches of obligations; unfair treatment; avoidable delays; failure to follow proper procedures; rudeness or discourtesy; not explaining matters; and poor or incompetent service.

[23]Ombudsman Services: Energy Report (2015) from my project: https://www.law.ox.ac.uk/sites/files/oxlaw/oxford_report_os-e.pdf.

In contrast to the ADR setting in Germany and its general acceptance through the lens of the formal justice architecture, the ADR tradition in the UK is different. There is not much documented trust in the justice system and the courts are unreachable for low-value consumer complaints. The public's relationship with the authority residing in the formal justice system, therefore, is not robust, indeed, it contains elements of scepticism and distrust. The ADR system (unlike its German counterpart) is therefore set up in such a manner as to provide a service that is non-legalistic, uses simple language and measures its decisions against what is fair and reasonable.

Conclusions

In this chapter I have discussed the implementation of the consumer ADR directive into national legal spaces. This legislation is very recent and, thus, most EU systems and their users need to be aware of, and get used to, this developing regime. Every member state has its own traditions and legal systems that have formed their populations' approaches to disputes, attitudes to institutions and expectations of those institutions. I have therefore argued that the relationships we form with authorities influence the relationships discussed in this chapter: specifically, those between the citizen and the state and those between the consumer and the business. These relationships are established and develop through our legal culture.

At the national level, for the purposes of this study, I suggest that legal culture can be understood as a mixture of its institutional infrastructure and people's consciousness. Put differently, legal culture is so much more than its legal institutions. Legal culture has to include the effect its institutions have on people who are part of the system, as well as how the people, in turn, make sense of the system. This boils down to people's relationship with the law being shaped by their experiences with and expectations of the institutions and authorities they encounter.

To recognize our constantly shifting relationship with authorities allows for the next layer of inquiry and a closer examination of the national infrastructure into which ADR is embedded. Acknowledging that there are many layers of justice systems and approaches within any country, I have focused here on the predominant national legal system into which ADR has been introduced as a means for accessible justice. The foundations have now been laid to address—in the empirical Chapters 5 and 6—the questions posed at the start of this chapter in relation to how the ombudsman model has different sets of meanings in different national contexts.

As mentioned above, this field of inquiry is in its infancy with its own literature only now starting to develop. In order to explore whether ADR is creating its own culture of legality, or whether it should be seen in the shadow of other legal authorities, I can offer a start to the debate through hypothesizing here that our expectations of ADR are closely interwoven with our national socialization towards institutions of the justice system. Adding to this, exploring the question as to why people would respect an ADR outcome and follow the decisions handed down (procedural justice) will provide a valuable insight into the ADR process. The next chapter will outline the accompanying theories of legal socialization and procedural justice.

4

Procedural Justice and Legal Consciousness: Questions of Theory and Method

Introduction

This chapter explains how I used a combined approach to theory and method. My starting point involved taking already established theories which explain why people obey the law and follow decisions handed down by authorities and applying these theories to a new context and discipline. This in itself was a huge challenge as theories come with their own complex sets of methods for exploring the context in question through quantifiable elements (specifically designed survey questions).

To this end, a survey was designed that incorporated all the necessary features for successfully capturing attitudes towards ombudsmen in various European countries. An initial look at the results offered by the quantitative data seemed only to relate to part of a more complex story. The data provided measurements of recent interactions expressing participants' expectations towards the ombudsman procedure. However, this snapshot of a moment in time needed to be supplemented by a theory that allowed reflection upon, and theorizing about, how the more complex parts of the stories, leading up to those moments, had come about. At this point, I decided that the use of qualitative considerations would enrich my analytical framework.

The problem of combining substantive concerns about the role of law in social life with the empirical analysis of human behaviour in rule-governed settings can be addressed by concepts of legal socialization and legal consciousness. These theories assist the analysis (see Chapter 6) by shedding light on the complex narratives that people construct to make sense of the

N. Creutzfeldt, *Ombudsmen and ADR*, Palgrave Socio-Legal Studies,
https://doi.org/10.1007/978-3-319-78807-4_4

law in everyday encounters. The combination of quantifying antecedents of procedural justice, on the one hand, and the study of how national behavioural responses are learned and have developed, on the other, form the mixed-methods approach that I will discuss in this chapter.

Readers will recall that the broader context of this study is the informal justice system, one of the functions of which is to provide dispute resolution through alternative pathways to the formal court system. Alternative dispute resolution (ADR) takes many forms and has a variety of meanings in different contexts (Menkel-Meadow 2010). In this book I am taking the ombudsman institution, as a provider of ADR in the informal justice system, as the unit of analysis. If we can understand people's encounters with and expectations of the informal justice system, we can then extract lessons about the institutions within it and thus inquire into institutional trust and legitimacy. This is especially important as researchers currently have little empirical understanding of users' encounters with the informal justice system. Questions therefore arise about whether different forms of justice systems should be evaluated by different user criteria? What do participants want and expect from ADR bodies? How are trust and legitimacy established in a 'developing institution'?[1] My aim is to combine inquiry about the role of law in everyday life in a given society in general, and the empirical analysis of human behaviour in rule-governed settings in particular. For this purpose, to explore people's attitudes towards ombudsmen, I engage with classic theories of trust and fairness and examine whether, and to what extent, they can be translated to the informal justice system in general and to informal dispute resolution systems in particular.

The Research Puzzle: How Theory and Method Can Learn to Collaborate

When trying to measure people's perceptions of an ombudsman procedure, fairness and trust are significant indicators. The theory of procedural justice, as described by Tyler and others (Tyler and Huo 2002; Tyler 2006), is the theoretical starting point for this study. I will explore this in more detail below. What is important at this stage is to grasp the basic notion that Tyler found empirical evidence for: people accept outcomes that were not in their favour if the procedure leading up to the outcome was experienced as fair.

[1]Chapter 7, drawing on the data and claims developed in this project, will attempt to answer the question of whether informal justice systems (ombudsmen/ADR) generate their own norms of fairness or borrow them from other systems.

Table 4.1 Ombudsmen annual reports on overall satisfaction and outcome

'*... it is undeniable that case outcome has a close relationship with satisfaction levels.*' Legal Ombudsman Annual Report 14/15
'*... the role of the final outcome is important, it is a driver of dissatisfaction, not delight.*' Local Government Ombudsman Annual Report 2007
'*... the procedure could not be separated from the outcome.*' IPSOS MORI Report 2010
'*There is a strong relationship between customer satisfaction and whether or not a case is upheld. For example, 80% of customers whose complaint we upheld were satisfied with our service. In contrast, customer satisfaction where we did not uphold their complaint was 53%.*' Parliamentary and Health Services Ombudsman Annual Report 2013
'*This shows how people's perception of our service tends to be influenced by how they see the outcome of their own complaint. Even so, many of those people who didn't get the outcome they had hoped for still expressed some positive views about their experience of bringing a complaint to us.*' Financial Ombudsman Services Annual Report 2013/14
'*It should be noted that outcome satisfaction is higher among those experiencing mutually acceptable settlement. This is likely to enhance views on other elements of service delivery and to be at least in part responsible for improving satisfaction with the outcomes achieved. 57% of Ombudsman Services customers were satisfied with the outcome achieved compared to 41% in 2013/14.*' Ombudsman Services Annual Report 2015

The elements that create those fairness perceptions in a procedure are: 'having a voice'; 'being treated with respect'; 'neutrality of person'; and 'being listened to' (Blader and Tyler 2003). This perceived fairness contributes to people attributing trust and legitimacy to that institution and thereby being more likely to follow its decisions.

Here the puzzle begins. Annual reports of ombudsmen state clearly, in their consumer satisfaction reports, that the outcome a person receives from their case determines their overall experience with the ADR provider. This suggests that people's perceptions of ombudsmen are primarily influenced by the outcomes they receive (some examples from the UK sample[2] are in Table 4.1). This impression was also confirmed when I asked at the 2013 Ombudsman Association annual meeting, by show of hands, how many in the audience (a mix of about 200 ombudsmen and complaint handlers) thought that the outcome people receive from them determines their overall impression of the procedure. Most of them thought the outcome was all that mattered for users' satisfaction.

[2]The UK ombudsman bodies have customer satisfaction data in their annual reports, whereas German and French bodies report on levels of consumer satisfaction, but do not ask about outcomes.

These extracts about consumer satisfaction from annual reports suggest that the majority of consumers cannot see the fairness of a procedure independently of their received outcome; the outcome frames their perception of the whole procedure. These initial discoveries led me to believe that further exploration was needed. There is no common method of data collection and evaluation amongst the ombudsmen; this makes the data that is available non-comparable. The question is: why does the data collected from the ombudsmen annual reports suggest such a different story to that described in the literature on procedural justice? There are at least three aspects to consider:

1. the different contexts and settings of the ombudsmen;
2. the method of data collection; and
3. procedural issues (expectations management).

Firstly, the typical forums for procedural justice inquiries have been courts, tribunals, the police, and organisational settings. The ombudsman context is different from the more formal settings and procedures of encounters with the police or courts. The ombudsman is a specific model of dispute resolution, more hybrid in structure. There is usually no face-to-face contact between the consumer and the complaint handler/ombudsman. In addition, the financial value of a case and personal investment in it are generally lower in a private ombudsman procedure than in a tribunal, court case or police interaction. The studied context also sets itself apart from a focus on organizational settings as my interest here is not in understanding how the ombudsman as an organization works, rather what the users expect of the procedures.

Secondly, the way the data is collected and analysed for the individual ombudsmen's annual reports is not standardised and therefore measures criteria in different ways. As such, both the quality and level of analysis varies greatly, as does the terminology (Doyle et al. 2014).

Thirdly, an ombudsman procedure does not usually require an independent lawyer or advocate (this might vary, in Germany it is not unusual to have a lawyer contact the ombudsman on the customer's behalf) who manages people's expectations throughout the process. This, amongst other things, has an influence on the consumer's expectations of what an ombudsman procedure can, and cannot, provide. Of course, moving away from hypothesis and theoretical considerations, when dealing with everyday situations boundaries become blurred and matters become entangled and complicated. The ombudsman institutions in this study vary in all sorts of ways: their local and national contexts; the nature of cases under their jurisdiction; and their mandates and powers (see Chapter 3). This is where theory needs to be complemented carefully by the right method. I believe that through a combination of quantitative and qualitative approaches, the context of the ombudsmen examined in this study can be understood in a productive way.

User data extracted from ombudsmen's annual reports generates *assumptions* that the outcome of an ombudsman procedure is the most important issue and that this outcome directly effects decision acceptance. This is also what people often assume about formal justice systems. How can we tell if there is a difference, not only between systems but also between process and outcome?

Discovering Similarities and Differences

Quantitative Measures

My main research tool, a survey, asked a range of questions about consumers' complaint journeys and their perceptions of the fairness of that process. This satisfaction survey was carefully designed to test quantitatively for procedural justice and legitimacy measures, as explained in the preceding section (and see the example survey in Annex 1).

The overall dataset consists of 2777 responses to customer satisfaction surveys (UK: 1310; and Germany: 1467).

Typically, ombudsmen send out their own satisfaction surveys to their users and report highlights thereof in their annual reviews.[3] There is no streamlined methodology or style for these surveys. Therefore it has been impossible to date to compare ombudsmen reports and performance against one another. My survey was the first consistent approach to measuring people's expectations and satisfaction levels with ombudsmen across sectors and countries.

Between September 2014 and March 2015 ombudsman staff sent out online and paper-based surveys to consumers who had recently been through their complaints procedures. In order to maintain the anonymity

[3]At the time of my study none of the German ombudsmen were sending out satisfaction surveys. As part of the ADR directives regular reporting requirements they then used the survey developed for this study as a template.

of the respondents and to prevent selection bias, I chose to ask the ombudsmen to send the survey to either all of their users who had recently completed a complaints procedure, or to a random sample of those who had recently completed a complaints procedure (depending on their respective caseloads). The survey clearly indicated that it was an independent study. I am sure that I would never have been able to gain access to the users (because of data protection rules) or have had such a good overall response rate if the ombudsman had not agreed to send out the online link and postal survey for my study. The survey was designed to produce robust information through attention to detail and ensuring that individual questions were relevant, unbiased and precise. I included measures of procedural justice and legitimacy in building the questions for the survey, working closely with leading academics in the field of procedural justice research and survey design to produce a suitable research tool. The survey is made up of a combination of closed questions (choice categories, Likert-style scale, checklists and rankings) and open questions (see Annex 1). The survey was piloted and fine-tuned before being distributed by the ombudsmen. Through these means the aim of designing a survey that would work in different settings and countries was accomplished.

Anonymous responses were received through the Bristol Online Survey (BOS) platform that I used to administer all my surveys. Returned anonymous postal surveys were added to the online system so that, at the end of the data collection period, all information was online. There are 2776 responses in the German and UK dataset with an average response rate of 22%. The response rates varied by ADR body (see Table 4.2), however, I did receive enough responses to make robust qualitative and quantitative claims.

When conducting surveys such as the one described here, there is always a risk of getting the timing wrong. There are also risks of receiving responses from individuals who are either upset with the system and want to vent their frustration, at one extreme, or those who are highly content, at the other (Fowler 1995). This cannot really be avoided in such a large project and does have the beauty of providing a rich database of people expressing strong feelings about the procedures. In fact, I did find a good balance had been achieved between respondents in the final dataset. For the statistical analysis the dataset was weighted to reflect the actual frequency of cases for each of the ADR providers. This involved collating data on the frequency of cases from annual reports, calculating the relative proportion of each scheme and weighting the dataset to reflect these proportions.

Table 4.2 Overview of ADR providers and responses

Ombudsmen	Surveys sent out		Responses to survey
	Online	Paper-based	
UNITED KINGDOM			
Parliamentary and Health Services Ombudsman	1.660	N/A	272
Local Government Ombudsman	673	164	316
Legal Ombudsman	200	N/A	52
Financial Ombudsman Services	1.334	N/A	195
Ombudsman Services: Energy	3.250	N/A	421
Ombudsman Services: Communications	314	N/A	50
Ombudsman Services: Property	32	N/A	4
GERMANY			
Petitionsausschuss	[a]	N/A	25
Schlichtungsstelle für den öffentlichen Personenverkehr (transport)	2.894	N/A	579
Schlichtungsstelle Energie (energy)	1.280	320	322
Schlichtungsstelle Telekom (comms)	150	N/A	26
Versicherungsombudsmann (insurance)	N/A	1.500	514

[a]This is an online service and a link to my survey was made available on their platform

Qualitative Measures

The qualitative dataset is a combination of the responses to the open-ended survey questions, interviews and focus groups. In addition, listening in on calls received by ombudsmen staff helped me to collect supporting material for the narratives I found in the open-ended survey responses.

As mentioned above, the open-ended questions in the survey asked about people's expectations of the ombudsmen and reasons for contacting them. The answers to these questions provide an unexpectedly rich qualitative dataset. Initially, the open-ended questions were added as an experiment to see if people would choose to take time to elaborate on their experiences, as well as ticking boxes for the quantitative series of questions. They did—the resulting wealth of data enabled me to explore, distinguish, and compare respondents' attitudes towards ombudsmen. Reading through thousands of responses I detected distinct similarities and differences in the emerging narratives.

Despite not having asked explicitly about how *the law* mattered when engaging with an ombudsman, the story that emerged from the data was one of complex attitudes to justice and provided an opportunity to explore legal consciousness as a lens through which to understand my dataset and suggest that, as a complement to the quantitative dataset, it gives the study a solid methodological grounding. In other words, combining quantitative approaches to procedural justice and building on them through qualitative insights offers a theoretical lens and a methodological tool that helps uncover people's expectations of institutions of informal justice.

Finally, interviews and focus groups with ombudsmen and their staff were conducted to add an extra layer of depth to the research. Before I designed the survey I held one focus group in the UK and one in Germany with the participating ombudsmen to get their views on consumers' journeys and experiences with them. After designing the survey I went back to each of the ombudsmen to discuss it and also to discuss the methodology of dissemination. Then, after the survey had closed, I again met up with all the participating ombudsmen to discuss the results.

In order to secure a better understanding of complaints procedures and the incoming survey data, I listened in on some of the calls that ombudsmen staff were taking at the Financial Ombudsman Service, Ombudsman Services and the Schlichtungsstelle für den öffentlichen Personenverkehr. I also talked to some of the complaint-handling staff about their experiences and had several (lengthy) phone conversations with (elderly) complainants to the Local Government Ombudsman.[4]

The datasets I collected were analysed to understand more fully self-reported experiences with, and expectations of, ombudsman's complaints procedures. As mentioned above, the lack of a streamlined approach to and consistency of data collection across the ombudsmen makes it impossible to draw precise comparative conclusions without a shared methodological approach. However, my study did apply a consistent approach in data collection and analysis across all ombudsmen in this project. The theoretical foundations that will be used to interpret the data are procedural justice, legal consciousness and legal socialization. I deal with these in the remainder of this chapter.

[4]In accordance with good academic practice and the ESRC requirements for grant holders this project received ethics clearance at the University of Oxford.

Procedural Justice

The theory of procedural justice seeks to explain what motivates people to obey the law (Hough and Tyler 2015). This body of literature originates from the field of experimental social psychology and investigates the influence of evaluations of how decisions are made. Assembling concepts from sociology, economics, criminology and political science Tyler (2006) and his colleagues produced the widely accepted argument[5] that people comply with the law out of more than just fear of punishment or self-interested motives. Procedural justice theory has been applied to and tested most comprehensively in policing (Tyler and Folger 1980; Tyler and Huo 2002; Jackson et al. 2011), courts (Lind et al. 1980) and organisational settings (Hofstede 1980; Greenberg Folger 1983; Van den Bos and Vermunt 1997).

The main focus of work on procedural justice has been to discover why people comply willingly with authorities and what criteria they use to assess the fairness of a procedure (Tyler 1988). Compliance is explained by the values of law being incorporated into people's own value systems, therefore according the law legitimacy. This means that procedural fairness and how an authority treats the individual are essential to its legitimacy.

People all have a notion of what a justice system is, with courts and police forming a significant part of it. Furthermore, people all have an understanding and acceptance of these institutions as representative of legal authority. This attitude of acceptance and conditioning does not seem to apply to an ombudsman, although the model has been a longstanding part of justice systems around the world. There is generally a low level of awareness and use of the ombudsman system. This raises questions of where an ombudsman is situated within the value system of the people and prompts a related question about the system's legitimacy. Furthermore, does the type of procedure have an impact on people's perceptions and, if so, why (Leung and Lind 1986)?

The key concepts of procedural justice, when applied to the ombudsman setting, can help detect the importance of procedural fairness in the context of a procedure aimed at settlement. There has been some research applying procedural justice theory to different techniques of ADR (Vidmar 1992). This research found that there are some preferences for the authoritative procedures of adjudication and arbitration over mediation and negotiation.

[5]And perhaps counter-intuitive? Or at least not immediately obvious.

Why do people sometimes prefer formal procedures over informal equivalents? Is this related to the nature of the conflict, the ritual of a formal hearing, or case-specific factors giving rise to judgments of procedural justice? Is procedural justice more important for people who lose their case? Further questions remain about the meaning of procedural fairness for different types of procedures. Is there a difference in the perception of fairness relating to a procedure that is aimed at settlement and compromise rather than judgment and determination (Lind et al. 1990; Jones and O'Flynn 2013)?

Procedural Justice in Different Settings

In the context of dispute resolution, Thibaut and Walker (1975) found that people's satisfaction with decisions is influenced by their judgements about the fairness of the dispute resolution process. This has been widely supported by subsequent studies in different settings (Lind and Earley 1992): on legal trial procedures (Lind et al. 1980); non-trial procedures (Casper et al. 1988); mediation (Lind et al. 1990); and organisational (Greenberg and Tyler 1987), political (Tyler and Caine 1981), interpersonal (Barrett-Howard and Tyler, 1986) and educational settings (Tyler and Caine 1981). There is widespread opinion that those affected by the decisions of third parties in both formal and informal settings react to the procedural justice of the decision-making process at least as much as and often more than they react to the decision itself (Lind and Tyler 1988; Tyler 1996).

Much procedural justice research has focused on translating Tyler's model to different settings—groups of people in different regulatory contexts and countries. The model focuses on non-instrumental aspects of procedural justice, in which process fairness and respectful treatment is presented as more important than outcome favourability for improving perceptions of legitimacy and subsequent cooperation with authority.

Following Tyler's model, can we assume that it is also applicable to informal justice settings? Will procedural justice prove important and be a predictor of decision acceptance? If we were to follow this line of reasoning, it would mean we can assume that, if people perceive an ombudsman procedure to be fair, this helps build the legitimacy of the institution. Correspondingly, people would therefore be more likely to trust the institution and follow the suggested outcomes. Several questions arise from this proposition. Does the model of procedural justice extend to a procedure that is inquisitorial by nature and aims for a settlement as outcome rather than a judgment; a model that is not bound by formal rules and is more flexible and informal (Bercovitch and Houston 1985)? Can findings from the late-1980s

American model of ADR—disputants have feelings of control and fairness, perceive the procedures and solutions to have greater legitimacy, and are more likely to comply with the terms of the conflict resolution decision (Welsh 2002)—apply to the European model of ADR (ombudsmen)?

To be able to empirically grasp the elements of procedural justice and test if they are applicable to the studied ombudsman context, the underlying concept, that of fairness, needs to be deconstructed.

Disentangling Perceptions for Empirical Analysis

The effects of procedural justice have been theorised from various angles. Early theories have an instrumental approach and see fair procedures as important because they lead to fair outcomes (Thibaut and Walker 1975). People evaluate fairness of a procedure in relation to the perceived fairness of the outcome. Thus, if the procedure is perceived as fair, the decision is more likely to be accepted as fair.

In contrast to this, relational, social-identity and group-value-based models describe how fair procedures have implications for social identity and membership in a social group or relationship with the group authorities (Lind and Tyler 1988; Tyler 1989; Hough et al. 2013). These approaches argue that procedural fairness is important for relational reasons, independent of the fairness of outcomes. Fairness heuristic and uncertainty models focus on the role that a fair procedure plays in the development of fairness judgments and how interactions with authorities are managed (Lind 1994), highlighting the importance of fair procedures relative to fair outcomes (Lind 1995).

Social psychology approaches to procedural justice conclude that the importance of procedural justice criteria varies depending on the situation or the procedure's social context. Thibaut and Walker (1975) describe four factors that affect preference for dispute resolution procedures:

1. the *nature of the conflict*;
2. the *time available*;
3. the *existence of a standard*; and
4. *outcome correspondence.*

Lind (1995) found that uncertainty about outcome justice might increase the importance of procedural fairness in evaluating it because procedural evaluation serves as a shortcut for making more complex outcome judgments. The social identity-based model (Tyler and Smith 1999) states that people place more importance on the quality of treatment when they identify themselves more strongly with the social group that the authority represents. The uncertainty management model put forward by (Van den Bos and Lind 2002) supports the thesis that fairness of a procedure matters more in situations where people have less information about the trustworthiness of the interacting authority.

Public Trust and Institutional Legitimacy

We can intuitively recognise that trust and legitimacy are important, but what establishes trust and legitimacy is a much more complex question. And further, how can we capture these concepts empirically? A starting point is to look at measures of *public trust in justice* and *institutional legitimacy* (Hawdon 2008).

Borrowed from procedural justice literature on policing, we can say that the need for justice institutions (ombudsman) to produce fair and respectful procedures—in contrast to their outcomes—is the safest strategy for building trust in justice, and thus institutional legitimacy and compliance with the law (Hough et al. 2013). Consequently, procedural justice and moral alignment are the most critical factors in fostering or retaining institutional legitimacy, albeit with perceived obligation and consent to legal authority also playing a role—winning the 'hearts and minds' is central to the effective use of authority (Jackson et al. 2011).

The concepts of legitimacy and trust provide connections between citizens and social systems (Jackson et al. 2011). The distinctions between the two concepts are adopted from the FIDUCIA report (Jackson et al. 2013) on comparative public attitudes towards legal authorities:

- *legitimacy*—a belief in the moral right of legal authorities to possess and exercise power and influence;
- *trust*—a belief in how individual actors working for the institutions perform their role (ibid.).

Following this definition, the measures of those concepts are proposed as follows.

- To measure legitimacy: the focus needs to be on judgments regarding the right of the decision-maker to prescribe behaviour and enforce laws that emanate from the role and institution. This translates into the ombudsman context: authority of the institution and individuals' (working for the ombudsman) moral validity.

- To measure trust: the focus needs to be on the intentions and capabilities of specific actors. In the ombudsman context the question asked is 'Can a procedure be trusted to both fulfil functions of fairness and effectiveness, and be dependable?'

The next section will explain how legitimacy and trust have been approached and measured in studies on public attitudes to date, in order to contextualise discussions for this study.

Legitimacy as an Empirical Concept

Tyler differentiates between instrumental and normative models of compliance with the law. The normative model is based on personal morality and legitimacy; detailed in the model of process-based regulation (Tyler and Huo 2002; Tyler 2003; Bottoms and Tankebe 2012). Here, procedural elements are measured by the quality of decision-making and the quality of treatment. According to this approach, described in the context of policing, the fairness of procedures that people experience have both immediate and long-term effects on their behaviours and perceptions (Tyler 2003). Thus, people's evaluations about the legitimacy of an institution are affected by the fairness of the procedures—more specifically, by the quality of interpersonal treatment and the quality of decision-making. If people feel that an institution is legitimate they are more inclined to feel an obligation and responsibility to cooperate with that authority.

Within this concept, Tyler (2003) emphasises the importance of procedural justice, as opposed to outcome justice, in shaping institutional legitimacy. In other words, perceptions of procedural justice and legitimacy result in everyday compliance with the law. Following Tyler's argument then, legitimacy is won and lost partly through the experience of procedural justice and injustice. Other scholars have described conditions that need to be met for an authority to have legitimacy. These are, according to Beetham (1991):

1. the obligation to obey;
2. legality; and
3. moral alignment.

Jackson et al. (2011) state that procedural justice and moral alignment are the most critical factors in fostering or retaining institutional legitimacy. However, a feeling of obligation and consent to legal authority also play a role. Hough et al. (2011) found that fairness and effectiveness are preconditions of empirical legitimacy.

An amalgamation of the above describes institutional legitimacy as the right to rule and the recognition by the ruled of that right (Coicaud 2002; Tyler 2006; Bottoms and Tankebe 2012). Building on these concepts, Tankebe (2012) defined legitimacy—in the context of policing—as made up of:

1. public perceptions of procedural fairness;
2. distributive fairness (or outcome justice);
3. effectiveness; and
4. lawfulness (or legality).

In summary, the development of understanding how legitimacy is empirically defined has many layers. As a starting point for the purpose of this study, legitimacy is empirically measured by the experience of procedural justice and injustice through the concepts identified by Beetham and Tankebe above. The survey was designed, with these concepts in mind, to explore ombudsman's legitimacy. This leads to the next question of trust. If authorities are seen to be unfair and disrespectful this damages trust in them.

Trust in (Informal) Justice

Trust in the procedural fairness of an institution directs attention to the ways in which institutions exercise their authority (Tyler 2006). Do ombudsmen treat people with dignity and respect? Do they make fair, transparent and accountable decisions? Trust relates to assumptions and beliefs about intentions (Do ombudsmen want to be fair?) and competence (Are they able to be fair?). Trust is about both present and future behaviour. This might be the distinction between the concepts of legitimacy and trust—where legitimacy is focused on the present, trust tends to be future-oriented and may be defined as a 'positive feeling of expectation regarding another's future actions'.

Tyler and Huo (2002) described this in their concept of 'motive-based trust'. People are more willing to defer voluntarily to authorities whose motives they trust. Tyler and Huo found that the influence of trust is independent of the favourability or desirability of the decisions the authority makes. They measured trust through the following indicators:

- the authority considered my views;
- tried hard to do the right thing by me;

- cared about my concerns;
- tried to take my needs into account.

These factors were used to measure trust in institutions about which people already had an opinion and experience. Institutional trust has been described as a 'system-level' public attitude. It is likely to reflect orientations towards organisations that are fairly stable. People's views on the police or courts, for example, are not in a state of constant flux (Bradford and Jackson 2010). This is very different for the ombudsman institution. We know that most people are not aware of it. How can institutional trust be built and measured in a developing institution?

To measure people's perceptions of trust and legitimacy in ombudsmen, I started from the criteria applied in the European Social Survey (ESS)[6] (a combination of Tyler and Beetham) as follows:

1. trust in justice institutions (effectiveness, procedural fairness, distributive fairness); and
2. perceived legitimacy (sense of obligation to obey, moral alignment, perceived legality).

To sum up, the theory of procedural justice provides us with measures to explore what motivates people to follow decisions, accept them, and trust the authority that issues them. To gain a fuller explanation and understanding of the context from which individuals form their attitudes and expectations towards authorities, legal socialization and legal consciousness are helpful.

Legal Socialization and Legal Consciousness

There are reasons why we expect certain outcomes from an authority/institution. I have argued above that people's expectations and acceptance of an informal justice system are based on experiencing a fair procedure (Tyler 2006). However, this is only one aspect of the complex set of expectations that shape people's relationships with informal justice systems. Generally speaking, these experiences are informed by people's legal socialization through national and cultural contexts developed when

[6]ESS http://www.europeansocialsurvey.org/data/themes.html?t=justice.

growing up. Legal socialization influences how we expect (legal) authorities to make decisions, how those authorities should treat us, and our beliefs about the boundaries of legal authority. Legal socialization is the process through which individuals acquire attitudes and beliefs about the law, legal authorities and legal institutions. This occurs through individuals' interactions, both personal and indirect, with police, courts and other legal actors.

To start to understand people's values of law and how they are formed we need to delve into the literature on people's experiences with an authority and how this is influenced by their habituated leaning (Tapp and Kohlberg 1971). Individuals' legal reasoning and their relationship with the law can be seen through the process of legal socialization (Tapp and Levine 1974). Legal socialization motivates people to form attitudes that reflect evaluations and expectations of a system and its institutions. These attitudes develop within a culture and can have quite distinct features. To detect cultural specificities and to get a deeper understanding of how people make sense of interactions with alternatives to formal legality, I consider the literature on legal consciousness (Merry 1990; Ewick and Silbey 1998; Halliday and Morgan 2013) to be very helpful.

Legality and legal consciousness have been described in various contexts, with different meanings in the literature. Legality, broadly defined, goes beyond what people label as legal. I am using this idea in an extensive sense to encompass attitudes to ombudsmen. Studies of legal consciousness have, to date, focused on people's encounters with the formal legal system and their reactions to it (Merry 1990; Ewick and Silbey 1998). My aim is to bring this literature to a new context and explore the consciousness around alternatives to formal legality, as legality constructs ideas about justice (Gill and Creutzfeldt 2017).

The complex interactions between power, resistance and deference are a central theme in legal consciousness research. Ewick and Silbey (1998) establish an analytical framework that provides three clusters or types of legal consciousness; they provide us with 'a cultural toolkit from which popular understandings of legality are constructed' (Silbey 2005: 349). The three types are: 'before the law' (impressed with it and convinced of its legitimacy); 'with the law' (utilizing it instrumentally and generally understanding law as a game); and 'against the law' (cynical about its legitimacy and distrustful of its implementation). These three schemas have since been supplemented by 'under the law' (the law is vehemently rejected and broken) (Fritzvold 2009). Further to this, Halliday and Morgan (2013) exposed the political dimensions of resistance, by drawing on Mary Douglas' (1992) cultural theory and adding a dimension of 'collective dissent' to the analytical framework.[7]

The study of legal consciousness has been developed in settings and situations where researchers are interested in understanding how people relate to law. Exploring citizens' encounters with public bureaucracies (Cowan 2004; Lens 2007) and understanding workplace grievances (Hoffmann 2003), the study of legal consciousness is moving slowly beyond its traditional confines. The ombudsman context, as part of the informal system, provides an interesting and unexpectedly fertile ground to develop the notion of legal consciousness. I propose to extend the legal consciousness scholarship and offer to refine it in two further ways: first, through looking at a particular institutional context and, second, through a comparison across cultures. I do this by using the framework of legal consciousness and extending it with a focus on exploring legality, fairness and legitimacy, with a shift towards symbols of law and legal authority. I propose to move beyond the aforementioned traditional confines and to explore the evidence the data affords, providing both common and distinct roles and narratives across countries. This approach explores the social meanings of ombudsmen and helps us understand where people place ombudsmen in the justice system. This method has uncovered role expectations and narratives in the dataset (discussed in Chapter 6).

What shapes our complex relationships with law? Legal socialization develops conceptions of the purpose and function of the law within society (Louin-Tapp 1991), meaning expectations of how actors in the legal system ought to fulfil their roles. These expectations inform notions of justice and fair play (Tyler 2009). Legal attitudes are created though legal socialization and those attitudes, I argue, can form the blueprint of people's expectations of the informal system.

Another dimension of socialization and consciousness happens at the cultural level. Here, the concepts of legal consciousness and legal socialization are used to explain both how individuals become attached to a culture and how the culture and institutions of a society are then maintained over time (Almond and Verba 2015). At this interchange of culture, its institutions

[7]In a previous paper we used the framework of legal consciousness to explore people's actions in response to dissatisfaction with the ombudsman (Gill and Creutzfeldt 2017). Our analysis of a distinct group of activists, whom we call the 'ombudsman watchers', are matched with the defining characteristics of an added dimension to Ewick and Silbey's (1998) types of legal consciousness, that of collective dissent (Morgan and Kuch 2015: 567). Whilst our paper focused on a particular group of ombudsman users that turned their grievances into an organized form of protest and activism, this book focuses on the everyday users of the ombudsman to explore specific characteristics and narratives.

and our learned behaviour is precisely where my overarching argument lies. The connection between our learned behaviours when encountering authorities informs and shapes our attitudes towards, and expectations of, other institutions of a system. Within this, there are culturally specific approaches (see Chapter 6).

Conclusions

With the stated aim of exploring how trust and legitimacy are constructed in a system that provides alternatives to formal legality, this chapter has provided an overview of how I negotiated theory and methods in this study. I chose a mixed-methods approach to develop a deeper understanding of how people relate to ombudsman procedures and to explore what they expect from them. My theoretical considerations were motivated by questioning results of satisfaction surveys in ombudsmen annual reports, finding that users mostly evaluate these services through the outcome they receive. This made me curious as to the perceptions of process; don't they matter in this context? To test this I looked at established theories of procedural justice that suggest that people can separate the procedural experiences from the outcome they receive and this contributes to the perceived legitimacy of the institution. The literature also suggests methods to test these phenomena. I designed a survey to measure antecedents of procedural justice in the ombudsman context in two countries. Here, my aim was to extend existing literature to a new context and explore consciousness around alternatives to formal legality, as legality constructs ideas about justice. To achieve this, I looked to theories of legal socialization and legal consciousness to grasp a fuller picture of the complex relationship people have with institutions that provide dispute resolution. This combination of theory and methods allowed the study to uncover culturally distinct differences in people's approaches to ombudsmen that will be discussed in following chapters. The questions that were posed at the outset of the chapter will accompany us throughout the empirical Chapters (5 and 6) that follow: namely, is there a difference in the perception of fairness relating to a procedure that is aimed at settlement and compromise rather than judgment and determination? And are there culturally distinct patterns of disputing behaviour?

Part II

Empirical Discoveries

5

Expectations and Perceptions of Ombudsmen in a Cross-National Comparison

Introduction

This chapter discusses the quantitative findings about people's attitudes towards an ombudsman. This study tests, for the first time, Tyler's psychological model of procedural justice in the ombudsman context and across countries. Tyler examined the general question of *Why People Obey the Law* (Tyler 2006) whereas, here I am aspiring to come closer to answering the question of why people are willing to follow ombudsmen decisions and, if not, why not; or, more modestly, to understand what motivates people to accept the outcome they have been given after completing an ombudsman process.[1]

The first step is to apply Tyler's model to the new context. Much empirical evidence points towards the importance of trust and legitimacy in generating acceptance of the decisions made by legal authorities. Moreover, people seem to be more attuned to the quality of the process concerned rather than the outcome it delivers. The procedural fairness of legal authorities—the extent to which they make decisions in an unbiased fashion and adhere to principles of dignity, respect and voice—has consistently been found to be a more important predictor of trust, legitimacy and decision-acceptance than the outcomes they provide (Blader and Tyler 2003;

[1]This study does not look at situations where people have been unwilling to accept a decision or even those, which might have led to legal proceedings. The responses were collected anonymously so I could not locate this data. Additionally, ombudsmen usually do not follow up if their decisions have been acted upon (those that have been accepted or not).

N. Creutzfeldt, *Ombudsmen and ADR*, Palgrave Socio-Legal Studies,
https://doi.org/10.1007/978-3-319-78807-4_5

Bradford et al. 2013; Hough et al. 2013). Here the social, cultural and practical power of the institutions might have an influence on perceptions of procedural fairness (Creutzfeldt and Bradford 2016). However, hardly any attention has been paid to institutions that provide informal dispute resolution across cultures. Is Tyler's model transferable into a new context institutionally, that of ombudsmen?

Taking a new approach to the literature on procedural justice, I explore the significance of associations found between fairness, outcome-acceptance, legitimacy and trust, as widely described in the context of policing and criminal justice (Bradford et al. 2013, Chapter 4). A brief recap of the individual concepts follows to assist the associations made in the cross-national comparisons.

Why does fairness matter to how we think about authorities? It is because, if people think that authorities are fair, it helps to secure a long-term commitment to the rule of law (Hough et al. 2013: 8). Additionally, if people perceive an authority to be fair, impartial and transparent in their procedures, it will secure support for and cooperation with those authorities (Hough et al. 2013). This means that perceived fair treatment promotes satisfaction with the authority and this enhances its legitimacy (Hough et al. 2013). Applied to the ombudsman context, if users perceive the interaction as fair, it will assist their commitment to the institution.

Legitimacy is related to authority. When people see a system as legitimate they recognise its authority (Beetham 1991). Awarding legitimacy to institutions is to grant them the right to exist, the right to determine authority and the right to exert power (Hough et al. 2013). This sentiment makes people cooperate with legitimate authorities because they feel it is the right thing to do (Tyler 2006). Legitimacy has been empirically captured as moral alignment, having a sense of shared values with the institution, and perceived legality (see this chapter). In other words, legitimacy finds everyday expression in people's sense that they are under a moral obligation to comply with a decision handed down by an authority and to comply with the law. This means that, if people feel that an ombudsman is legitimate, then they are more inclined to feel an obligation towards it and a responsibility to cooperate with its decisions. Users are also more likely to accept decisions, not least because these are experienced as 'right and proper' when handed down by a legitimate authority (Tyler and Rasinski 1991; Tyler 2003). This suggests that legitimacy as well as procedural justice can provide useful insights when examining people's responses to decisions handed down by legal and quasi-legal authorities. If legitimacy then refers to a fundamental property of legal and quasi-legal institutions (Gill and Creutzfeldt 2017), the right to govern, and the recognition by the governed of that right (Jackson et al. 2011), how do these apply to the ombudsman context and how does it manifest itself within diverse cultural settings?

Public trust is extremely difficult to grasp empirically. Trust always involves a 'leap of faith' (Möllering 2006), which can happen at any moment in time and in any circumstance. Trust is also a practical matter, relating closely to notions of accountability (O'Neill 2002). Moving from the abstract to the tangible, we can quantify trust through how individuals working for institutions perform their role. Here, we could ask what generates trust and thereby capture it empirically as a combination of fair and respectful treatment and decision-making (Tyler's process-based model) (Blader and Tyler 2003). Extensive research in the field of policing suggests that people base their trust judgements in part on what the authority actually does (Bradford et al. 2013). In my study this translates into an exploration of how individual actors working for ombudsman institutions perform their role. This will be discussed in this chapter and the next, informed by the quantitative and qualitative dataset. The aim of the chapters is to offer different theoretical lenses to makes sense of the empirical dataset, exploring people's fairness perceptions, trust and the perceived legitimacy of ombudsmen across national boundaries.

This chapter is divided into three parts. The first discusses national patterns and cross-national comparisons of the private ombudsman sample in Germany and the UK.[2] The second provides an overview of the public–private divide in the UK. In part three I revisit relationships, through the national lenses that shape our interactions with ombudsmen.

Detecting National Patterns and Cross-National Comparisons

Recall the overarching research question: what are the predictors of perceptions of procedural justice during the process of dealing with an ombudsman and what factors shape outcome-acceptance by complainants? My aim here is to detect cultural similarities and differences that became apparent when analysing the database. To achieve this aim, the data is divided into

[2] I chose this approach to reflect the national patterns of people approaching ombudsmen/ADR in general, rather than looking at each sector individually. German sample (VO, SÖP, SChliT, SChliE); UK sample (OS:E, OS:P, OS:C, FOS, LeO).

two sets to answer the research question. The first set of data consists of the private ombudsmen in the German and UK database. Although different types of ombudsmen make up the respective country databases, I combine all the people using private sector ombudsmen in the analysis. I chose this approach to reflect the national patterns of people approaching ombudsmen/ADR in general, rather than looking at each sector individually (this I do elsewhere: Creutzfeldt 2016a; Bradford and Creutzfeldt 2018). This data elicits general national patterns.

The second set of data consists of the UK sample only, investigating national details by comparing users' fairness perceptions of public and private ombudsmen. Asking the same questions about procedural justice and outcome-acceptance in the national context uncovers another layer of complexities within the ombudsman landscape. The scope of this book is not to focus on the intricate differences between each individual or sectorial ombudsman model, but rather to provide an empirical base from which to understand people's motivations and attitudes towards ombudsmen in general.[3] Much scholarly attention has already been paid to examining the development of individual ombudsmen, mainly in the public sector (Behrens 2012; O'Brien 2015).

Analysing Fairness Judgements

Tables 5.1, 5.2, 5.3, 5.4, 5.5, and 5.6 are cross-tabulations and highlight the similarities and differences found when comparing the two countries. With a focus on the motivations to complain and the willingness to accept a decision, culturally distinct patterns are highlighted.

Regression analysis was used to probe further the factors shaping people's overall fairness judgements (Table 5.7). The response variable was the single item, which gauged respondents' overall perception of the fairness of the process. This was a ordinal indicator measured on a five-point Likert-type scale, with higher scores indicating more favourable views; ordinal logistic regression was therefore the preferred analysis technique.

Four variables were included as predictors of overall fairness judgements. First, two scales of procedural justice were created, representing respondents' views of the fairness of interpersonal interaction (or treatment) and

[3]It is too soon to understand fully the implication the ADR directive has had on the national private ADR bodies. Similarly, the UK public sector ombudsmen are undergoing significant change which requires some time to see the effects.

Table 5.1 Motivations for the complaint—procedural justice-related concerns

	Most important	Important	Neutral	Not very important	Least important	$Chi^2(df=8)$	*p*
Getting someone to listen							
UK	56	19	12	3	10	38.2	<.0005
Germany	49	17	20	6	7		
Getting an apology							
UK	28	20	22	11	18	209.3	<.0005
Germany	13	6	23	15	42		
Being treated with respect and dignity							
UK	47	23	16	5	8	64.5	<.0005
Germany	31	21	24	9	15		
To get an impartial view							
UK	57	17	11	6	10	29.3	<.0005
Germany	61	18	13	3	5		

Table 5.2 Motivations for the complaint—outcome-related concerns

	Most important	Important	Neutral	Not very important	Least important	$Chi^2(df=8)$	*p*
Resolving my problem							
UK	85	3	2	1	9	111.8	<.0005
Germany	89	5	4	0	1		
Getting my money back							
UK	48	15	17	7	14	157.9	<.0005
Germany	74	9	10	2	5		
To get what was lawfully mine							
UK	48	14	15	6	17	173.0	<.0005
Germany	68	15	11	2	3		

Table 5.3 Motivations for the complaint—change-related concerns

	Most important	Important	Neutral	Not very Important	Least important	$Chi^2(df=8)$	*p*
Changing the business process							
UK	40	19	18	8	14	56.2	<.0005
Germany	25	19	28	10	18		
Preventing others having the same problem							
UK	53	18	13	6	10	95.6	<.0005
Germany	32	22	26	8	11		

Table 5.4 Willingness to accept the decision—outcome favourability

	Willingness to accept decision					
	Willing	Neither	Unwilling	*n* (=100%)	$Chi^2(df=2)$	*p*
Outcome favourable						
UK	95	2	3	449	12	<.0005
Germany	98	1	1	955		
Outcome partially favourable						
UK	54	17	30	84	23.6	<.0005
Germany	80	14	6	129		
Outcome not favourable						
UK	12	14	74	146	28.8	<.0005
Germany	36	12	52	325		

Table 5.5 Willingness to accept the decision—fairness of the procedure

	Willingness to accept decision					
	Willing	Neither	Unwilling	*n* (=100%)	$Chi^2(df=2)$	*p*
Procedure fair						
UK	94	4	3	441	0.2	0.895
Germany	94	4	2	1155		
Not sure whether procedure was fair						
UK	58	17	26	139	13.4	<.0005
Germany	40	15	45	191		
Procedure unfair						
UK	6	15	79	141	5.4	0.068
Germany	6	5	88	95		

Table 5.6 Willingness to accept the decision

	Willingness to accept decision					
	Willing	Neither	Unwilling	*n* (=100%)	$Chi^2(df=2)$	*p*
UK	69	8	22	721	35.6	<.0005
Germany	81	5	14	1441		
	Outcome favourability					
	Favourable	Partially	Unfavourable	*n* (=100%)	$Chi^2(df=2)$	p
UK	66	12	22	679	5.3	0.07
Germany	68	9	23	1409		
	Fairness of the procedure					
	Fair	Not sure	Unfair	*n* (=100%)	$Chi^2(df=2)$	p
UK	61	19	20	722	108.5	<.0005
Germany	80	13	7	1441		

Table 5.7 Ordinal logistic regression models predicting judgement of the overall fairness of the procedure (high scores = more fair)

	Model 1		Model 2		Model 3		Model 4		Model 5	
	ß	se(ß)	ß	se(ß)	ß	se(ß)	ß	se(ß)	ß	se(ß)
Country (ref: UK)										
Germany	0.54***	−0.11	0.74***	−0.18	0.74***	−0.18	0.24	−0.19	0.30+	−0.16
Distributive justice (ref: no)										
Yes	0.53***	−0.12	0.52***	−0.12	0.52***	−0.12	0.25	−0.18	0.54***	−0.12
Outcome favourable? (ref: no)										
Yes	2.26***	−0.12	2.25***	−0.12	2.25***	−0.12	2.26***	−0.12	1.94***	−0.18
Procedural justice										
Quality of treatment	0.01	−0.04	0.07	−0.06	0.07	−0.06	0.02	−0.04	0.02	−0.04
Quality of decision-making	0.36***	−0.02	0.36***	−0.02	0.36***	−0.02	0.36***	−0.02	0.36***	−0.02
Interactions										
Treatment* Germany			−0.09	−0.07						
Decision-making* Germany					−0.09	−0.07				
Distributive justice* Germany							0.46*	−0.23		
Outcome favourability* Germany									0.47*	−0.21
N	2158		2158		2158		2158		2158	

+p < .1; *p < .05; **p < .01; ***p < .001

the fairness of decision-making. Fairness of interpersonal interaction was measured by taking the sum of four binary indicators which asked whether the people respondents first spoke to in relation to their case were helpful, treated them with respect, seemed well intentioned and seemed interested in what they had to say (mean = 2; SD = 1.6; min = 0; max = 4). Higher scores on this scale indicate a more favourable view of the quality of treatment. Fairness of decision-making was measured by taking the sum of five items, measured on five-point Likert-type scales, which asked respondents their views about whether the ombudsman kept their word, had the authority to help, were easy to get in touch with (i.e. open), knew what they were talking about, and acted impartially (Cronbach's alpha = .93). Higher scores on this scale indicated more favourable views (mean = 19.4; SD = 5.5; min = 5; max = 25).

Other constructs were included in the model as binary (dummy) indicators. Perceived distributive justice was measured by a single item indicating whether the respondent believed that others in a similar situation would receive the same outcome as themselves. Outcome favourability was similarly measured by a single item indicating whether the respondent thought that the outcome was in their favour.

Finally, a dummy variable was included that indicated whether the respondent lived in Germany or the UK.

People's Fairness Perceptions in Germany and the UK

Following the method of analysis described above, this part presents data for the two country case studies. It seeks to answer the questions: *what motivates people to complain to the ombudsman* and *how willing are respondents to accept a decision*? The answers to these questions are presented in Tables 5.1, 5.2, 5.3, 5.4, 5.5, and 5.6.

Motivation to Complain

Table 5.1 shows the different motivations for bringing a complaint to an ombudsman. We can see that for UK respondents three of the four procedural justice-related concerns were *most important* (56% getting someone to listen to me; 47% to be treated with respect and dignity; 28% getting an apology) compared to German respondents. For both German and UK respondents it was important to get an impartial view (61 and 57%). Further, 42% of German respondents thought getting an apology was the least important motivation for their complaint, compared with 18% of UK respondents.

Table 5.2 shows that German respondents tended to be more focused on getting their money back (74%) and to get what was lawfully theirs (68%) as an outcome-related concern. UK respondents, in comparison, did not place as much weight on those factors.

Table 5.3 shows that for UK respondents a motivation to complain was changing the business process (40%) and preventing others from having the same problem as themselves (53%). For German respondents, these matters were not such important drivers to complain.

Tables 5.1, 5.2, and 5.3 show distinctions in the comparison between UK and German respondents in the importance of procedural justice-related concerns, outcome-related concerns and change-related concerns. Summing up, procedural justice measures seem more important factors in raising complaints for UK respondents than for German respondents. For German respondents, the most important outcomes were to be given what was owed financially, based on what they felt was their legal right.

The next set of data illustrates what factors drive the willingness to accept a decision. Here, outcome favourability and perceived fairness of procedure are measured in relation to the willingness to accept a decision.

Willingness to Accept a Decision

Tables 5.4, 5.5, and 5.6 show what motivates respondents to accept a decision. Table 5.4 shows that 80% of the German respondents are willing to accept a decision if the outcome is partially in their favour (as opposed to 54% of UK respondents). Interestingly enough, 36% of German respondents are also willing to accept the decision if the outcome is not in their favour (12% UK).

Table 5.5 shows that both German and UK respondents were willing to accept a decision if they thought it was fair (94%) and unwilling to accept it when they felt it was unfair (German 88% and UK 79%). This is what we would expect. What the data further reveals is that 58% of UK respondents who were not sure if the procedure was fair were still willing to accept the decision, compared to 40% of German respondents.

Table 5.6 shows that 81% of German respondents were willing to accept the decision, 68% had a favourable outcome and 80% thought the process was fair. In comparison to the UK respondents where 69% reported a willingness to accept the decision, 66% had a favourable outcome and 61% thought the process was fair.

Thus, Tables 5.4, 5.5, and 5.6 show that German respondents are more likely to accept a decision if the outcome is partially or not in their favour than are the UK respondents. Overall, German respondents reported a higher willingness to accept the decision than UK respondents.

To recap, whilst finding similarities in people's motivations to complain to an ombudsman and their willingness to accept the decisions, the data shows country-specific propensities. However, as the sample consists of a mix of different ombudsmen in each country, we cannot therefore identify here specific trends for financial ombudsman users, or energy ombudsman users, for example. The aim is to understand what people who complain to an ADR body expect from the process. These expectations are of course also conditioned by the nature of the process and what people know about it. To be able to explore further the national propensities detected, the following part models judgement of the overall fairness of the procedure in an ordinal logistic regression.

Culturally Specific Patterns

Results from the ordinal regression models are presented in Table 5.7. Five models are shown: Model 1 includes just the main effects, while Models 2–5 add, in turn, the interaction between country and each of the four main predictors. This allows consideration of whether the importance of distributive justice (for example) as a predictor of overall fairness judgements varies between the UK and Germany. The regression coefficients in ordinal logistic regression models can be interpreted in terms of the probability of moving up (or down) the response scale. A positive coefficient indicates that higher scores on the explanatory variable (more procedural justice, believing the process was distributively fair, receiving a favourable outcome) were associated with a higher probability of higher scores on the response variable—that is, more perceived overall fairness. Conversely, a negative coefficient indicates that higher scores on the explanatory variable were associated with a lower probability of higher scores on the response variable (less perceived overall fairness).

Model 1 shows that procedural justice—in the form of judgements about the fairness of decision-making—distributive justice and outcome favourability all contribute to overall fairness judgements. Conditioning on these other factors, there is no independent association between the fairness of interpersonal interaction and overall fairness. Yet, holding all other variables constant, German respondents were more likely to judge the overall process fair. This can be illustrated in terms of fitted probabilities generated from the model. Holding all other variables at their mean, the probability of a German respondent believing the overall process was 'very fair' was 0.59, while the probability of a UK respondent who made similar judgements about procedural and distributive justice and outcome favourability believing the overall process was 'very fair' was 0.52. This may indicate that there are shared national specific expectations towards the ombudsman process. Two questions follow this assumption: what motivates German participants to think processes are fair and accept them even if they don't get the outcome they wanted? Second, what motivates UK respondents to place more weight on the fairness of a process compared to the German sample? A broad analysis and explanation of these propensities will be offered in Chapter 6, drawing upon theories of legal consciousness and legal socialization to help understand what drives people to reach decisions about what they perceive as fair and reasonable.

Models 2–5 expose further propensities by showing that German respondents tended to place more weight on distributive justice (Model 4) and outcome favourability (Model 5) when forming their overall fairness judgements; however, the relative importance of procedural justice concerns did not seem to vary by country. Similar to the cross-tabulations in Tables 5.1, 5.2, 5.3, 5.4, 5.5, and 5.6 a distinction is apparent here between the German and UK respondents. Why is it that German respondents care more about the financial outcome and the legality of a process, whereas the UK respondents seem to care more about a fair process and how their case might assist others in their complaint? The quantitative data has made it possible to demonstrate empirically that procedural justice matters in the context studied across countries. It did also, however, show that there are differences. These differences most definitely have a multitude of explanations, but I argue that understanding cultural influences can help grasp these national distinctions and start to explore how to maximize the effectiveness of procedures and the quality of the experience for the specific audience. Also, taking cultural considerations as a starting point allows us to reflect upon the context into which the ombudsman has been placed.

Do ombudsmen represent a social category with which people feel an association, and which they feel is important? If ombudsmen do not have this representational quality then the association between procedural justice and legitimacy, and the outcomes of that association (such as decision-acceptance), may be weaker than is commonly found elsewhere. Procedural justice has been found to strengthen the social bonds between authorities and subordinates which link it to legitimacy, cooperation, decision-acceptance and compliance (e.g. Tyler and Blader 2000; Bradford 2014). I found that outcome favourability predicted perceptions of procedural justice to a larger extent than is often found elsewhere, for example, in the courts and police. One possible explanation for this is relates to complainants' lack of experience with ombudsmen, as mentioned above. It also chimes with van den Bos et al.'s (1997) findings that, if people are not sure about what to expect from a process, the perceived fairness of the outcome has more weight in their assessment of the fairness of the process. We also found that a range of other factors are important in the ombudsman context to predict decision-acceptance independent of procedural justice, for example, receiving an unexpected outcome.

This raises questions as to where ombudsmen are situated within people's value systems, and whether norms of procedural justice figure as prominently in people's evaluations of ombudsmen behaviour as they do in, for example, their evaluations of the behaviour of police officers. On a more fundamental level, the type of procedure under consideration may have an impact on people's perceptions of its fairness and on which aspects of the process figure most prominently in their assessments of it (Leung and Lind 1986). It may simply be that people conceive of their interactions with ombudsmen in a different way to their interactions with more established legal authorities, such as police officers and judges, who, not coincidently, wield far greater symbolic and literal power over them. We might speculate, then, that the modal interaction between members of the public and an ombudsman service will be more transactional in nature than that between a citizen and a police officer or court official. Many people who contact ombudsman services wish simply to get a refund from a goods or service provider they feel has not lived up to expectations (see Table 5.2). Taking this into consideration, might the legitimacy of the ombudsman have a different set of preconditions, given that people may approach the ombudsman not for justice but for a purely instrumental return ('getting their money back')? Studies within the procedural justice literature regularly contrast instrumental against affective or relational 'drivers' of legitimacy, decision-acceptance and other outcomes, and most conclude that affective, process-based concerns are, on average, more important (Creutzfeldt and Bradford 2016).

The results show that people's overall perceptions of the case in which they were involved, and of the ombudsman service concerned, are influenced by perceptions of both process and outcome. If people get the outcome they expect from an ombudsman, they think the procedure is fair and will then accept the decision they have been given. But, equally, if they feel the process was conducted in a fair manner they are also more likely to accept the decision even if it went against them. Of course, there are many factors that motivate people to accept an ombudsman decisions. The results show procedural justice effects are important in the context studied. Looking into more detail, moving from the country comparison to the national level, we can uncover more divisions in the public and private sphere.

Public Sector Ombudsmen in the Administrative Justice System in the UK

Having compared national clusters and identified patterns of selected private sector ombudsmen in the UK and Germany, I would like to draw some attention to the national context. In order to examine more closely the national architecture of ombudsmen, it is necessary to draw upon the set of UK data alone (as mentioned above)[4] which includes two UK public sector ombudsmen and five private sector ombudsmen. The focus here is to compare the ombudsmen operating in the civil justice system, as per the first part of this chapter, with the ombudsmen in the administrative justice system. The starting point is procedural justice and decision-acceptance among users of private and public ombudsmen in the UK.

What type of interaction do users have with ombudsmen? As stated above, ombudsmen are not as high profile as are, for example, the more traditional aspects of our legal system, such as police officers, lawyers, judges or the courts (see Chapter 1). A consequence of this is that people are not aware of what ombudsmen do and what purpose they serve or what outcomes they can provide. Users of ombudsmen therefore are still developing trust and negotiating legitimacy in the ombudsman institution. An ombudsman lacks the power over individuals, symbolic and literal, that a police officer or a judge has. This makes the interaction between people and an ombudsman more transactional in nature (Creutzfeldt and Bradford 2016).

People reach out to ombudsmen in the private sector if they encounter a contractual problem with a good or service they have purchased, whereas they approach a public sector ombudsman if they have encountered problems with a public service provider (Chapter 3). At this initial stage, there are different drivers to complain and different expectations that motivate

[4]The UK dataset consists of 1306 responses. Public sector: PHSO $n=272$, LGO $n=316$; private sector: FOS $n=195$, OS (property, comms, energy) $n=475$, LeO $n=52$. Unfortunately I was not able to run my survey with the French *defensor des droites*, and the German *Petitionsausschuss* did not return enough surveys to make meaningful and valid claims.

people. For example, getting a refund or compensation is the main driver for people to complain about a private sector service, as seen in the data above. This might be seen as an instrumental return of 'getting their money back', rather than seeking to settle matters of justice. Whereas, on the other hand, seeking a systemic change and preventing others from having the same problem, is the most important motive for a participant bringing a complaint to the public ombudsman. A reason for this could be that public ombudsman services might be more closely linked to the state and, thus, be superordinate identities of the kind also associated with the police and courts. Users might feel a certain sense of entitlement to the service sorting out their problem. Private ombudsmen, however, may lack such associations since taxpayers do not typically fund them. Here, the fairness of their activity may be less identity-relevant to users of their services. These arguments will be revisited in Chapter 7.

In summary, results show that people's overall perceptions of the case in which they were involved, and of the ombudsmen concerned, are influenced by perceptions of both process and outcome. If people get the outcome they expect from an ombudsman, they think the procedure is fair and will then accept the decision they have been given. But, equally, if they feel the process was conducted in a fair manner, they are more likely to accept the decision even if it went against them. Procedural justice matters in our encounters with ombudsmen. Taking a closer look, the UK dataset uncovers a public/private divide see Figs. 5.1 and 5.2.

Figure 5.1 shows a summary of the answers to questions about perceived timeliness, transparency, fairness of the outcome, and the quality of communication. A clear division between public and private ombudsmen users can be seen. One of the implications of this is trust-related; it appears that people who use a public sector ombudsmen trust it less than those who use a private sector ombudsmen.

The data exposed a further example of the divide between public and private ombudsmen users related to legitimacy. Figure 5.2 summarizes the responses into public and private ombudsmen users. It is clear that the people who use private ombudsmen are more convinced that the ombudsmen are acting lawfully, have confidence in the ombudsmen, and feel a moral obligation to follow the decision.

Possible explanations for the expressed levels of dissatisfaction with the public sector ombudsmen lie in their changing role and a loss of trust by users.

The ombudsmen in the UK have been mainly associated with focusing on maladministration. This focus has now shifted towards an ombudsman

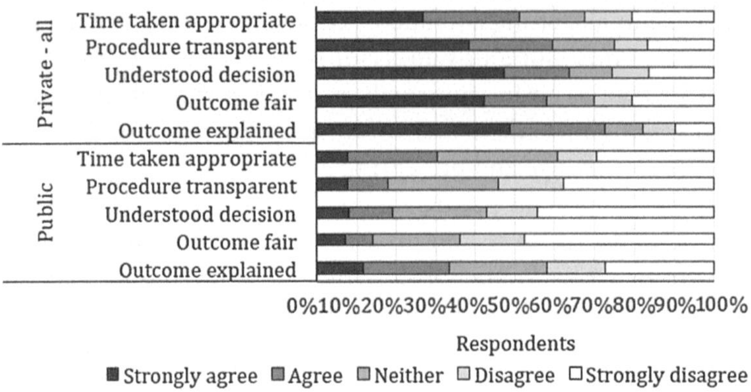

Fig. 5.1 Public–private divide: outcome-related

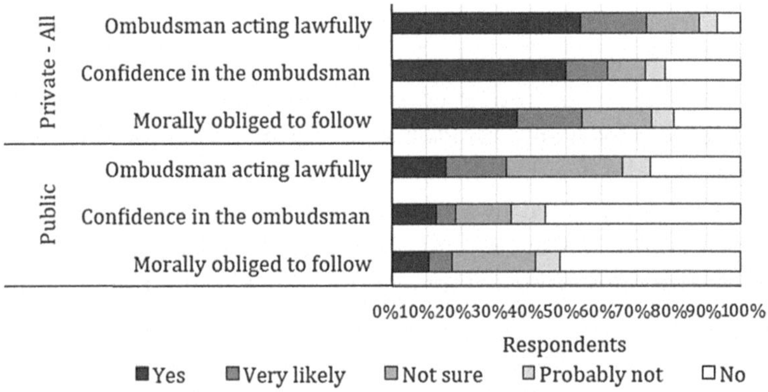

Fig. 5.2 Public–private divide: legitimacy

playing an active role in improving administrative decision-making. The administrative justice system has been shaken up by a wave of policy activity (Kirkham 2009; Gulland 2010; Mullen 2010; Buck et al. 2011; Adler 2013) focused on the relationship between redress mechanisms and administrative decision-making. The ombudsman is at a crossroads between improving the quality of administration as well as resolving individual disputes (Compton 1970; Clothier 1986; Parliamentary and Health Service Ombudsman 2009). Harlow and Rawlings (1984) refer to this as 'fire-watching' (improving administration) and 'fire-fighting' (redressing individual grievances). Traditionally, ombudsmen have focused on fire-fighting as one of their primary goals, but these vary according to the ombudsman service.

A loss of trust in public institutions goes hand in hand with the loss of trust in the ombudsman. Behrens (2015) attributes four key elements to public trust and the ombudsman. These are: first, 'perceived honesty and independence of a profession and the ability of professionals to make public interest decisions unsullied by vested interest or political interferences' (p. 4); second, no profession is trusted unless it demonstrates that it is trustworthy by serving its users and the wider public; third, the internal culture of high standards and transparency goes along with improving professional integrity and increasing confidence in public institutions; and, fourth, 'active trust' has to manifest itself through the people working for the public bodies and ombudsmen who must adopt the above-mentioned procedural justice criteria (treating people with respect and dignity, giving people voice, making them feel heard, and providing a neutral environment). Much attention has been paid to how, in the UK, all of these elements have been disrupted though reputational damage of institutions and professions. This has cast a long shadow on the institutions of public administration.

The public ombudsman plays a crucial role in translating the aims of the administrative justice system into everyday practice. The ombudsman's role in the administrative justice system is to *provide effective redress*, usually through recommending a win–win outcome. In this context, we need to be careful not to see the ombudsman in isolation but as part of an overarching system of redress.

The ombudsman plays a key role in promoting trust in public services and government (Creutzfeldt 2016d). To be able to fulfil this function, the ombudsman needs to be perceived as legitimate and be trusted by a range of parties. We need to understand key relationships in a person's complaint journey as a system of trust, taking restorative justice as an inspiration as a lens through which to understand these relationships. The main relationships are those between an individual, the public service provider and the ombudsman. I apply restorative justice approaches to recognize the cycle of a user's journey and its institutional connections. Some scholars have discussed the relevance of restorative justice to the civil justice system and ADR (Menkel-Meadow 2005). However, the connection to the administrative justice system and ombudsmen in particular has not been the subject of any detailed study as yet. Reinforcing voice and managing individual expectations prevent disengagement and thereby promote trust in the institution, in public service providers, and in government. This in turn will improve *active trust* and create trustworthy behaviour.

How can trust be maintained and built? In an ongoing effort, I suggest, it takes different approaches according to the circumstances. What is clear, however, is that by 'giving a voice to all parties affected, it reaffirms the moral and ethical aspect of the state and its institutions—it affirms the individual's relationship with the state not only on a rational level but also on a social and emotional level' (Gilad 2008). If this is applied throughout the institutions that a complainant deals with then a solid foundation of trust can be laid. How realistic this is, on the other hand, is another matter.

The notion of disentangling oneself from the ombudsman process in isolation, and understanding what happens before and after, allows us to recognize trust and legitimacy in its wider context. The discussion then focuses on institutions, authority and how we relate to them—a relationship with authority that we are constantly renegotiating, guided by our experiences. Another aspect that plays a significant role when we think about overarching relationships and engagement with institutions and authorities is that of the emotional cost to the individual.

Theoretically, we can easily predict what needs to be done to improve trust, legitimacy and fair treatment. However, the translation into everyday practice is somewhat challenging and directed by mundane realities like funding, staffing, training and wiliness to prioritise. The challenge is to translate what the data tells us about users' expectations into realistic everyday practice.

Re-evaluating Relationships through a National Lens

This part offers an initial reflection upon how we might relate from a national perspective to the concepts of fairness, legitimacy and trust discussed above.

At the outset of this chapter, I introduced different sets of relationships that influence our interactions with ombudsmen and used measures of established models tested in different contexts to explore why people obey (or disobey) the law. In this regard, procedural fairness and legitimacy are connected to people developing institutional trust. In the case of informal dispute resolution it is a novel inquiry. No scholarly attention has been given to how we make sense of institutions that are newly introduced into our justice system. The same questions apply in this context—what makes us accept a decision issued by an ombudsman and how do we develop trust and legitimacy in the bodies that are a new addition to our justice system? I propose the idea that in our judgements about the informal system we are influenced by our national legal culture and formal justice system. Our relationships with the state, authorities and the law (Braithwaite 2014) are shaped, amongst other things, by our upbringing and interactions with these institutions. Put differently, I suggest that our expectations are not formed by the informal system itself—due to lack of exposure and socialization (Chapter 6)—but, rather, they are guided by our pre-existing attitudes towards the formal system.

Based on the quantitative findings above, this chapter has looked at national patterns and started to unpack the relationships a bit more in preparation for the following chapter. As considered in this chapter, German legal culture is very different from its British counterpart. The extent of these differences lies in legal traditions and distinctive political and historical developments. They impact on how we make sense of, and relate to, our surrounding legal institutions. These differences are also expressed through legal language and its terminologies which shape the national debates around the role of the state, legality, legitimacy and fairness, for example. The discourse the language of legality provides allows us to apply it to other institutions until the time when ADR and ombudsman procedures might produce a vocabulary of their own. Meanwhile, the language of legality helps us to express a concept of fairness that is connected to the principles of law (Levine and Mellema 2001: 181). Different notions of rights rhetoric have evolved in Germany and the UK. Germans have a strong rights-based rhetoric whereas, in the UK, law and order competes with rights rhetoric (Lazarus 2004). Germans place high expectations on the government and the legal system. According to Damaška (1986), they believe in the state and trust government institutions and the knowhow of authority.

Compared to Germany, the UK has had historic continuity and relatively successful, if organic, democratic traditions, conventions and institutions (Lazarus 2004). Thus, British tradition does not possess such a symbolic significance, in contrast to German political and legal culture that can scarcely be disentangled from the country's political memory. In the UK, there is a pragmatic, empiricist and positivist idea of national rights and this arises with it a sceptical attitude toward idealist notions of national rights or 'comprehensive ideology of any kind' (see Lazarus 2004: 164; Jowell and Oliver 2007; Dagger 1994). The British legal system is accustomed to tradition and practical experience (Loughlin 1992). The desire of the British to be heard by authority is encapsulated in the cliché 'I want my day in court'.

The national lens allows us to shed some light upon how we develop our understanding and appreciation of the justice system. In this chapter, I have suggested that our notions of fairness, legitimacy and trust towards institutions and authority are generated by our environment. Building on the data presented above, we can see that German and British respondents, despite placing value on procedural justice, created their own distinct narratives. These narratives, explored in more detail in the next chapter, have their origins in our relationships with the law and authority. Before turning to a closer examination of some justifications for a national approach to dispute resolution in Chapter 6, I would like to offer some reflections on the natural boundaries of a purely quantitative inquiry.

Conclusions

I had to engage with quantitative methods for the first time when starting the project this book is based on. The result is that, not only am I in awe of anyone who finds joy and excitement in number-crunching, I also learned that there are many ways to approach large datasets. This dataset was analysed according to pre-existing and well-tested measures for enquiries into procedural justice and legitimacy, amongst other fields. Advice was also taken from leading experts in procedural justice research with regard to the running of regressions and manipulation of the multitude of variables with which I worked. I measured and tested for antecedents of procedural justice, as well as more general comparators. The results supported the initial hypotheses that, although procedural justice matters to all in the sample, there were distinct patterns in each country. This in itself is a valuable contribution to the procedural justice literature and the insight gained from quantitative analysis.

To be able to explain the differences found in the national datasets, it is necessary to move beyond statistical measures. As I suggest in the next chapter, we can add pieces to this puzzle by approaching the qualitative dataset through different theoretical lenses. This mixed-methods approach allows for an expansion of the inquiry to help make sense of respondents' self-reported perceptions and attitudes.

The aim of this chapter was twofold, first to empirically prove if procedural justice matters in the ombudsman context and, second, to uncover nationally distinct patterns. The data showed that procedural justice does matter in our interactions with the ombudsman, but also identified national propensities. It makes perfect sense that users desire to be treated fairly and be heard does not seem to be restricted by national borders. But how can the nationally specific patterns be explained? The quantitative dataset does not allow for more exploration about *why* these differences occur. These propensities, I have argued, are based on our nationally developed relationships with authority and our formal justice system. I am interested in how we make sense of those relationships and what makes us place our trust in institutions, mediated through fairness, legitimacy and the national context. A question might be whether ADR/ombudsmen generate their own norms of fairness or they are seen in the shadow of the law. To explore these notions further, I will draw upon the qualitative dataset to explore theories of legal socialization and legal consciousness.

6

Everyday Assumptions about Ombudsmen

Introduction

In Chapter 5, I discussed the quantitative dataset through the theoretical lens of procedural justice. The self-reported perceptions of recent users of ombudsmen procedures revealed that procedural justice matters across the dataset; however, some nationally distinct patterns were revealed. In order to explore these national distinctions, I now look at the qualitative data through the theoretical lens of legal consciousness. I argue that we need to go beyond a purely quantitative approach to appreciate the complexity of human decision-making and to understand how our behaviour is motivated by our attitudes. Legal consciousness provides the organizing theoretical framework through which I explore what motivates people to think and act the way they do when interacting with the justice system. Here, my contribution is an illustration of how legal consciousness and legal socialization matters in the ombudsman context, across countries. My reading of the data suggests that people's relationship with the formal legal system plays a crucial part in how they engage with, and make sense of, informal dispute resolution.

To explore this proposition, the intersection of legal socialization and the qualitative data provides fertile ground. Here, based on narratives of legal consciousness, role expectations towards ombudsmen are discussed. These roles are developed, refining a legal consciousness approach (Creutzfeldt 2016e) as cross-cultural narratives in the UK and German databases.

N. Creutzfeldt, *Ombudsmen and ADR*, Palgrave Socio-Legal Studies,
https://doi.org/10.1007/978-3-319-78807-4_6

I also extend the inquiry into a particular institutional context[1] and across cultures. This enables me to compare attitudes towards ombudsmen in different countries and to explore social meanings of ombudsmen. The data provided narratives for the role expectations and through the lens of legal socialization the roles will be anchored in their national context. It will provide more insight into how people relate to authority, as well as further investigating attitudes to fairness, legitimacy and trust. Are these attitudes borrowed from the formal legal system? Are they used as a benchmark to shape attitudes towards the informal system? Does ADR (ombudsman) create its own fairness and legitimacy?

This chapter is made up of four parts. First, cultural narratives are discussed through the lens of legal socialization. Second, the role expectations and assumptions about ombudsmen that the qualitative dataset has produced are outlined. Third, expectations of ombudsmen are discussed. Fourth, relationships to authority are examined in the context of roles and national narratives.

Interpreting Cultural Narratives

I explored in Chapter 4 how people form expectations of justice that an ombudsman can provide. Building on the theory of legal consciousness and legal socialization, I provide empirical support for my claim in this chapter.

How we relate to our national legal system and what we expect of it is formed through a complex process of legal socialization (Trinkner and Cohn 2014) and our experiences. Combined, these produce and shape our everyday attitudes towards the law, towards authority, and towards institutions, for example. Our expectations and images of the justice system and what it is supposed to provide for us informs how we make sense of institutions we are confronted with that we have not been exposed too before, such as an ombudsman.

Legal socialization influences how we expect (legal) authorities to make decisions, how those authorities should treat us, and our beliefs about the boundaries of legal authority. Further, legal socialization motivates people to form attitudes that reflect evaluations and expectations of a system and its

[1] I refer to the ombudsman as a single institutional context—one that can be contrasted with tribunals or courts. There is, of course, a range of both public and private ombudsmen and a more fine-grained analysis may reveal notable differences in users' perceptions of each of them. But there is analytical value in treating ombudsmen as a single institution and that is what I have done in this study.

institutions. These attitudes develop within a given culture and have distinct features. To detect cultural specificities and to gain a deeper understanding of how people make sense of interactions with alternatives to formal legality, I believe the developing field of legal consciousness (Merry 1990; Ewick and Silbey 1998; Halliday and Morgan 2013) is very helpful.

Through my approach of searching for experiences, understandings and clusters of meanings (Ewick and Silbey 1998), four roles became apparent in the data. These roles were generated by respondents' expectations and attitudes towards the ombudsman without any explicit questioning, or mention, about 'the law' in the survey. Following the methodological approach of legal consciousness studies, I was able to detect roles that feed into national narratives of expectations of informal justice, while guided by the ways law is experienced and understood by ordinary citizens (Merry 1985) and the terms in which people understand legality. According to Ewick and Silbey (1998: 35): 'In order to discover the presence and consequence of law in social relations, we must understand how legality is experienced and understood by ordinary people as they engage, avoid, or resist the law and legal meanings.' Translated to the ombudsman context and using legal consciousness as an organizing framework, we can now examine culturally specific accounts and expectations.

This chapter draws upon the German and UK dataset $n=2775$. In total, 1465 responded in the German sample and 1310 responded in the UK sample. The average response rate was 22%. The open-ended questions in the survey and interviews provide the data for this chapter. The open questions in the survey were:

- *Could you briefly state, in your own words, what the problem was you contacted the ombudsman about?*
- *What did you expect the ombudsman to do for you?*

Then, a few of the closed questions had an option to elaborate:

- *Were you satisfied with how the ombudsman dealt with your case?*
- *Was the way in which your case was handled what you expected?*
- *Do you have any other comments about the way in which the ombudsman service dealt with your case?* (see Appendix)

The range of responses allowed me to get a better and more nuanced understanding of respondents' attitudes towards ombudsmen. Complex attitudes to justice came to light and produced the four roles discussed later.

Interviews with ombudsmen in Germany and the UK supplement the dataset and provide a balance to the roles and narratives the qualitative dataset produced.

The sample consists of a specific kind of ombudsman user: someone who has recently experienced an ombudsman complaints procedure and chose to take part in this study. This raises the chances of those users that have strong feelings about their process being provided with another channel to voice their grievances, as well as positive experiences. Further, as mentioned before, the types of complaints that the ombudsmen in the sample deal with vary. This means that people will experience different sets of problems with varying importance and impact on their everyday lives. The data and type of study I undertook did not allow me to go into the detail of individual cases. I am more interested in getting a better understanding of how people engage with informal justice by managing their overall complaint and, in doing so, discover what role fairness, legitimacy and the formal justice system play. To achieve this, this study looks at general attitudes and detects patterns in complainants' expectations; it is not an in-depth case-by-case analysis.

What this chapter (or indeed this book) does not do is to dissect the dataset according to various sector-specific ombudsmen. I fully appreciate that a person turning to an energy ombudsman faces different sets of problems than a person who turns to a financial ombudsman. In this study I cannot determine, for example, the impact of the complaint on the complainant's life and the emotional cost. Therefore, I propose to contribute to a more general understanding of how people form their attitudes towards a system of justice in which they have not been socialized and find out how they make sense of what is fair, just and legitimate. In other words, I am interested in contributing to our understanding of the acceptance of institutions across cultures and to grasp how these institutions are made sense of and accepted in their national context.

Roles and Assumptions about Ombudsmen

I identified shared role expectations that users of ombudsmen have in the German and UK dataset (Table 6.1). People who interact with ombudsmen expect them to be interpreters, advocates, allies and instruments (Creutzfeldt 2016e). It became apparent that the roles are not completely separate from one another. Interestingly, the data shows that respondents can alternate between these role expectations during their complaint journey. Similar to other studies of human behaviour and everyday interactions, there can be no

Table 6.1 Normative roles that people expect of ombudsmen

INTERPRETER	• *... to help me understand what it's all about.*
ADVOCATE	• *...to hand over my problem.*
ALLY	• *... to share the responsibility.*
INSTRUMENT	• *...they have the right tools to help me.*

clearly defined boundaries. The identified roles help, however, to understand discrete stages of the complaint process that an individual is going through. The combination of roles and the shift between roles, amongst other things, provide evidence to support the emerging national narratives identified in the previous chapter. Building on Chapter 4's findings, the common starting point within the identified roles is the desire of the respondents to be heard, have a voice, and to interact with a person who has the capacity to act upon the imbalance of power between the individual and a business (private) or a state authority (public). The roles provide a set of expectations of the ombudsmen throughout the complaints process. The following sections will discuss the roles in turn and then deliberate upon how they help our understanding of attitudes towards ombudsmen and authority and what we might learn from this about the social meaning of ombudsmen.

Next, guided by the inquiry about how people who use ombudsmen make sense of that process, the four roles that evolved from the German and UK dataset are described (Table 6.1). The emphasis of my research is on users' attitudes towards ombudsmen (ADR system) and how these differ across countries. A detailed analysis of the differences between the individual ombudsmen deserves to be part of another study employing a different methodology (Creutzfeldt 2016c; Bradford and Creutzfeldt 2018). Here, I seek to explore how a model of justice—with the aim of improving access to justice—is perceived and used within a national context.

As mentioned above, there is no clear divide between the roles. They can be attributed individually, in a succession, or interchangeably according to the process. This mirrors not only the general lack of awareness of what an ombudsman can do, but also the complainant's learning process during a process. A significant influence upon the creation of the roles for ombudsmen is the exposure and experience a complainant has with an authority (see the later part of this chapter). Complainants appear to approach the ombudsmen with different sets of expectations. However the shared outcome amongst all users is the desire to solve their problem. The level of engagement the complainant chooses to have in this process varies. This variation is part of the role expectation, as shown below. Generally speaking, the roles indicate that some complainants appear to be more active in the way that they use the ombudsman as a means to get the outcome they anticipate (ally and instrument), while others are more passive and wish to hand over their problem to the ombudsman do deal with (interpreter and advocate).

Ombudsman as Interpreter

The concern of people who expect the ombudsman to be an interpreter is that of basic communication. It links to the findings in Chapter 5 that people who reach out to an ombudsman are in desperate need of being treated fairly, being taken seriously, and being given a voice. The user's expectation of the ombudsman to be an interpreter in the dataset follows. Some respondents don't know what to expect:

> I don't know really. Tell them off? Make them not do it again? I felt the energy company were so uninterested in my complaint that most people (esp vulnerable people or those with English as a second language) would never have got any sort of resolution. I hoped [the] Ombudsman would make them see the error of their ways.

Others were seeking a voice that reassessed the power imbalance and that they felt had got lost in the automated systems:

> I felt I was being ignored by the energy company and I hoped that they would have to take notice of the ombudsman therefore resolving my problem; I have been on hold with [energy provider] for 40 minutes on many occasions and in the end I realised that I haven't got time for it to go any longer. All I was hoping for the Ombudsman to do was to tell them to close my account—[energy provider] has ignored all of my emails and messages on Facebook so I had no other means of contacting them. [energy provider] owed me £270.

Others expected the ombudsman to 'to tell [energy provider] they were being unfair to the customer as they weren't listening to me', Some respondents simply wanted a response: '[to] get the government department to reply to my complaint letter'. Other respondents were keen to get an independent view of the case and some information about what to do next: 'I was hoping that PHSO could give me an independent view of my complaint and advice of the avenues available to me to pursue it further'; 'To be fair and consider the circumstances, and to take my human rights on board and liaise with me rather than paperwork from the banks which does not reflect the conversations they had with me.'

The examples show that the need for communication is twofold: on the one hand, complainants need to be supported to understand why their previous interaction with the company/public service provider did not resolve their grievance; and, on the other, they need to know how to enter into the process of the ombudsman assisting them in a complaints process. Here the main task of the ombudsman is to fix the broken-down communication and help the complainant understand what they can reasonably expect. This is a shared issue that all ombudsman institutions face. The staff that deal with complainants at first contact are typically the least well trained. If staff do not know in what emotional state complainants might be when first contacting the ombudsman and appreciate their heightened need for being heard (Creutzfeldt and Bradford 2016), then complainants are likely to face disappointment. In this regard, ombudsman have taken action and experimented with placing more experienced senior staff at the front-line which has provided for better consumer satisfaction and resolution of complaints at an early stage: According to the Financial Ombudsman Service (FOS): 'So often, this satisfaction is just a question of our being able to step in as early as possible – to talk people through the reasons and the complexities behind their problem.'[2]

Summing up, a complainant who approaches the ombudsman and expects them to be an interpreter is actually seeking clarification and basic guidance as to what the process can provide. One could argue that this underlines the findings about the importance of procedural justice described in Chapter 5.

Ombudsman as Advocate

The concern of people who expect ombudsmen to be their advocates is linked to the interpreter role discussed in the previous section. In a way, this role expectation is a step up from the basic seeking of understanding and making sense of the ombudsman process (interpreter). Here, an ombudsman as advocate is expected to act on the complainant's behalf and is handed the responsibility without much further input from the complainant: The role as a supporter is asking the ombudsman to fulfil a task of providing a voice for the consumer, to be a consumer advocate. The consumer is

[2]FOS Annual Review (2016: 6): http://www.financial-ombudsman.org.uk/publications/annual-review-2016/ar16.pdf.

expecting the ombudsman to support him/her in the complaints procedure. In this type of relationship, the complainant is reaching out to the ombudsman with a desire to hand over the problem, trusting that the ombudsman has the power to produce a positive outcome for them. This role, similar to the previous interpreter role, also comes with different levels of expectation. For example, some complainants were seeking 'to just get an apology for me', and for the ombudsman to 'intervene and apply common sense on my behalf'. The next level would be complainants hoping for 'advice on scale of compensation offered by [energy company] based on OS: E's experience'. In another example, the respondent said:

> I hoped that my problem would be brought to the attention of [company x] more forcefully than I was able to do. I felt as if I was just a number in the scheme of things and I should wait to be told at their convenience. I hoped they could provide an answer and a time scale to bring this to an end.

There is a strong propensity expressed in the data of respondents feeling voiceless and for the ombudsman to speak out for the complainant just to get through to the company or public service provider.

> I hoped they could get both companies to actually listen and properly investigate what was causing the delays so someone could take responsibility and finally sort it out, rather than just expecting me to pay money that I didn't actually owe at all. Neither company would listen to me and just kept telling me it was the other company's fault.

In another example, a complainant said: 'I expected the ombudsman to take an impartial view and assess whether the procedures had been properly followed. I also hoped that the Council would have been ordered to be more transparent in their dealing with the public.' Another wanted 'someone to look through my case and all the letters from physios, Dr's, Occupational Therapist and other healthcare professionals stating I need to be on the ground floor and help me to move'. And in one final example, the respondent said: 'I needed help to force [energy provider] to do something rather than totally ignore our complaints for many months.'

To sum up, a complainant who approaches the ombudsman expecting them to be an advocate is seeking to hand over their complaint. They do so in the hope that the ombudsman will have the voice and the power to actually get through to the company or public service provider that is being complained about. Complainants who wish the ombudsman to be their advocate are in some ways more proactive than those who seek interpretation. However, although this type of complainant has a clearer understanding of how the ombudsman can help them sort out the problem, they choose not to be actively engaged in the process.

Ombudsman as Ally

The *ombudsman as ally* is expected to be a professional and competent partner who stands by the complainant's side. The complainant needs backup, support, and reassurance. This role also includes the complainant handing over his/her problem to the capable hands of an ombudsman. Unlike the previous expectation of advocate, where the complainant plays a passive role, deeming the ombudsman to be an ally means there is a greater level of involvement from the complainant in the process. Put another way, the complainant actively seeks out the ombudsman as an ally—this perspective ties in directly with the imbalance of power and results in the complainant making use of the ombudsman to speak on their behalf.

For example, as one respondent commented: 'I do not see myself as a negotiator and have little experience of the financial world. I see the Financial Ombudsman Service as an independent body who I trusted to act on my behalf.' And: 'I expected the ombudsman to take my evidence and that of the Council to evaluate whether maladministration had occurred and to investigate the complaint thoroughly and provide my family with the opportunity to put forward our concerns.' Another said that they expected the ombudsman to 'facilitate transfer to new social work team, take disciplinary action against local authority and its employees over bully[ing] and harassment from social workers.' Other representative expectations towards an ombudsman as ally are: 'to realize that the "remedy" offered by the council was unacceptable to me and instruct the council to offer a better solution, which would not have affected the council in any way, but simply not allowed them to bully me.'

Similarly, fairness expectations run like a thread through all the roles, with different prominence: 'I expected the ombudsman to give a fair and proper judgement of my claim, regardless of the outcome being in my favour or not.' Another example: 'I expect fairness and help to sort out my complaint without bureaucracy and without having to take the formal legal route.' Likewise, complainants expected 'fast unbureaucratic help with an acceptable outcome, and help to enforce my request for compensation'.

A person who expects the ombudsman to be an ally is aware of what an ombudsman can do and is actively seeking help in jointly sorting out the problem.

Ombudsman as Instrument

People who expect the ombudsman to be an instrument are using the ADR route with knowledge and clear expectations of what the ombudsman can do for them. The complainant is well aware of what an ombudsman can do and uses this to their benefit. As with the previous roles, there are also different levels of expectations within this one, for example: 'As I felt I had given [energy provider] every opportunity to resolve the matter, I contacted the ombudsman in the hope that the meter would be changed before the start of winter as I do not want a huge heating bill.' And again: 'I expect the ombudsman to assist me in obtaining my case files regarding events fabricated by the inspector and to also hold the council accountable for the complete lack of service provided in addition to their extremely rude behaviour.' Some respondents were quite clear that they expected the ombudsman to 'bring the energy supplier to justice and get the problem sorted out to my satisfaction'. Others expected the ombudsman to 'step in promptly to stop this abuse of power and disregard for the accepted procedures by the District' and, further, to 'ensure the Local Authority complied with the law, apologised and corrected their procedures, which were proven, by independent investigators at Stage 2 of their own process and again at Complaints Panel (Stage 3) to be in error'.

On a more substantial level, complainants expected the ombudsman to bring about institutional change:

> I expected them to get the Council to change their policy so that other people didn't fall foul of it ... Also so that the Council would in future be taken seriously by local developers, builders and architects who currently lie in the application and development process knowing they can do so with impunity. I also hoped in the beginning that the Council would insist on my neighbours restoring the planting they had destroyed.

With a conviction to bring about change others stated:

> I ask for support to ensure that the highlighted problems are corrected to safeguard others ... Conduct a thorough investigation into my concerns so that lessons could be learned ... Investigate matters impartially and attempt to rectify wrongdoing by a public body and make recommendations to alter the bodies' structure accordingly.

Finally, a respondent insisted that: 'I hoped that they would have enough power to be able to make the bank review its customer service.'

The concerns of a person who expects the ombudsman to be an instrument are twofold. First, in comparison to the other roles, this person has clear outcome expectations and uses the ombudsman to realize them. Second, the person is aware that there is a problem with the system and seeks to redress not only their own personal grievance, but also to get the ombudsman to create change in the way the system works. Here, a divide between public and private sector users becomes apparent (Creutzfeldt 2016c; Creutzfeldt and Bradford 2016). The data clearly indicates that users of the public ombudsmen are more minded to address systemic issues and prevent others suffering from the same problems, whereas a typical user of the private ombudsmen in the dataset is rather, apparently, aiming for a financial refund and concerned about their individual complaint.

What Do We Expect of Ombudsmen?

The four roles that the dataset produced demonstrate a general absence of knowing what to expect of an ombudsman process. This comes as no surprise; unlike in Scandinavian countries and the Netherlands, where settlement and ADR are part of early socialization (Aleinikoff and Klusmeyer 2001), in many other European countries there is no established experience with ADR. The identified roles reflect users' varying levels of engagement with, and knowledge of, the ombudsman process.

Considering the four roles outlined above, I find that a complainant who expects an ombudsman to be an *interpreter* is looking for basic explanations, clarifications, and a level of communication that they have not managed to obtain from the business or public body complained about. For the ombudsman to fulfil this role, they need to be a good communicator, know what they are talking about, and manage expectations effectively. At that point the complainant can decide whether to move on to handing over their complaint to the ombudsman (*advocate*) or to take on a more proactive role in engaging in the complaints process (*ally* or *instrument*).

The expectations towards an ombudsman to be an *advocate* are those of handing the complaint over to be sorted out by a professional who has the skills, voice and power to get through to the company or public service provider. This type of complainant is slightly more engaged in wanting to go beyond communication barriers and towards the ombudsman in seeking explanations for the problem at hand. Thus, the complainant seeks to understand what the ombudsman can do to help, but chooses not to be involved in the process—instead transferring responsibility over to their advocate.

We now turn to individuals with expectations of the ombudsman being an *ally*. A person who expects the ombudsman to be an *ally* is more aware than those whose expectations are of allies or advocates. These complainants are actively seeking help to jointly resolve the problem. The ombudsman is expected to make an effort to form a united front against the company or business and to seek redress with an outcome about which the complainant already has strong views.

Lastly, a person who expects the ombudsman to fulfil the role of an *instrument* is clear about what an ombudsman can do and uses the service as a strategic tool to get a fair, fast, and efficient outcome. The ombudsman is one route to redress and as such needs to live up to the individuals' expectations (that in some cases might be unreasonable). In particular the role expectation of the ombudsman to be an *instrument* exposes the distinction between public and private sector users as found in the quantitative dataset in Chapter 5. The narrative that shapes this role develops around a shared, strong desire to put the problem right. Again it transpires, however, that there are distinctions between the users of public ombudsman and the users of private ombudsmen (Creutzfeldt 2016c). It appears to be most important for users of a private ombudsmen to get a fast resolution to their problem accompanied by a financial settlement. In contrast to this, a user of a public ombudsman seeks to set the problem right, for others as well, and wants to bring about a systemic change.

This analysis is, of course, using the idealised narratives of the data to highlight these differences. There are, as mentioned before, many reasons for these variations and not all are clear-cut in that people who contact the public ombudsman may also be seeking financial compensation and those contacting private ombudsman might also be hoping for systemic change. As stated before, I am merely highlighting trends in the data that will help identify our relationship to the ombudsman.

In sum, as was the case with the quantitative data in Chapter 5, the qualitative dataset provides evidence for common approaches to and expectations of ombudsmen, as well as national distinctions. The four roles, despite having no clear boundaries, show similar expectations across the dataset for those seeking *advocates* and *interpreters*, whereas distinct national characteristics can be discerned for the roles of *instrument* and *ally*.

Once I had examined more closely the roles of *ally* and *instrument*, it became possible to show how they differ between the UK and Germany, related to national characteristics that have been described as general legal culture and institutional availability (Creutzfeldt 2016e). I found that the roles of *interpreter* and *advocate* reflected a shared search for information and communication by complainants and portrayed individuals who, after reaching out to the ombudsman, preferred to hand over the problem. The roles of *ally* and *instrument* exposed a different, more actively engaged individual. An example of this distinction is the use of language when interacting with the ombudsman. In Germany (aligning with the national legal culture outlined in Chapter 2), the roles of *ally* and *instrument* tend to be framed in very legalistic terms. In the UK (again aligning with the legal culture described in Chapter 2), the expectation that the ombudsman fulfils the role of *ally* and *instrument* is expressed in narratives that are framed less legalistically, less formally.

In the next section, I explore the differences identified above by extending the deliberations to consider legal socialization when making sense of national distinctions. I believe the emerging differences in interactions are based on how individuals have learned to relate to authority and that this is shaped by our national legal socialization. It leads the discussion to the question about people's experiences with the law and authority, how this is influenced by their habitual learning (Tapp and Kohlberg 1971) and how this, in turn, shapes their interaction with the ombudsman.

Revisiting Relationships and National Narratives

I suggest that legal socialization can help us make sense of the interactions and expectations of the ombudsman as uncovered by the empirical data. Legal socialization is the process though which individuals acquire attitudes and beliefs about the law, legal authorities and legal institutions (Tapp and Kohlberg 1971). This process can be placed in the context of larger conceptions of legal culture, values, fairness, justice, legitimacy, and how we relate to authority (for example, Mill 1950; Friedman 1969; Rawls 1999; Tyler 2003). It allows me to extend the research for a better understanding of our relationships with fairness, legitimacy, and authority—and to situate it in the context of an ADR procedure.

Relationships with Authority

Legal socialization refers to the development of values, attitudes and behaviours towards the law. Tapp and Levine (1974) argue that it describes the individual's standards for making socio-legal judgments and for resolving conflicts, pressing claims, and settling disputes. This chimes with Friedman's

(1969) conception of legal cultures as the network of values and attitudes relating to law, which determines when and why and where people turn to law or government, or turn away. These broad conceptions help understand how we relate to the law through which channels this relationship is defined. The institutions of each legal system play a part in the socialization process: 'Most citizens acquire their notions of rules, laws, and obedience, and develop strategies for utilizing the law through, an interaction between natural cognitive structures and a host of "legal" environments such as the home, school, friendship circle, or court' (Tapp and Levine 1974: 4).

Legal socialization is closely linked to values we develop and it informs our actions. It is a process in which:

> … we acquire our legal values, such as fairness, equality, and justice, and our norms of rule-governed behavior. The primary socializers of legal values may be families, schools, peers, religious groups, or the state itself, depending on the relative influence of these agents in the culture and the extent to which a society is traditional in its orientation to authority. (Tapp and Levine 1974)

Here I leave the debate about when and how legal and political socialization takes place to others (Renshon 1977; Sigal 1989; Cohn and White 1990; Tyler 1990, 1994). The important issue for our purposes is that our legal values are shaped alongside our interactions with the law. This, in turn, will have an impact upon our perceptions of fairness and justice.

Closely linked to the above is the development of our sense of legitimacy. As discussed in Chapter 4 and empirically established in Chapter 5, literature on procedural justice and legitimacy have been linked to compliance and cooperation. Procedural justice appears to be integral in influencing perceptions of authority and views of legitimacy. The way people are treated by those in positions of authority can cause strong reactions and altered perceptions of legitimacy, not only of particular authority figures but also of the system they represent (Tyler and Huo 2002; Sunshine and Tyler 2003; Murphy and Tyler 2008; Bradford et al. 2009). In a longitudinal study, Kaiser (2016) found 'perceptions of procedural justice to be malleable. They can change over time and are influenced by a number of factors. Legal socialization beliefs, however, demonstrate only marginal change over time, suggesting these beliefs to be more stable.' Legal socialization directly influences how we view institutions and legal actors (Trinkner and Cohn 2014: 603). Our attitudes towards authority are thus heavily swayed by our legal socialization (Hyman 1959; Tapp and Levine

1974; Tyler 1994). In other words, one way to understand the arguably more changeable, context-specific and time-sensitive perceptions of procedural justice is to put it into perspective with a more enduring long-term process of legal socialization.

We internalize law-related norms in the process of legal socialisation. These are created though the fairness of authority and the development of positive orientations towards authority (Trinkner and Cohn 2014). This means that legal socialization is shaped through interactions and experiences with authority, as well as by the development of cognitive reasoning abilities (Tapp and Levine 1974). Our legal socialization typically happens in our national legal context, which means that we are programmed towards the legal culture in which we grow up and with which we interact. I argue that people tap into this programming when interacting with the informal justice system and people are faced with an ombudsman or other ADR provider. Consequently, people make use of their available information in their encounters with ombudsman. Put differently, I suggest that the relationships people form with the formal legal system direct their interactions with and expectations of the informal justice system. I discuss these next in their national context, guided by the roles the dataset provided, in the broader context of legal socialization.

In Chapter 2, I outlined the justice systems and accompanying legal cultures that shape the countries discussed in the book. Substantiating my argument with empirical data, I subsequently demonstrated how the concepts discussed in relation to legal socialization are relevant in the national context as shown in the roles the data provided. The relationships we form with authority, the state and the law are based on numerous considerations. It is impossible to trace specific orders or levels of importance between these elements. For the sake of exploring the national context, I now build upon the roles through the lens of legal socialization and offer an insight about the relationships discussed above. We negotiate our relationships with authority and the law through many facets of our daily lives, as well as through learned behaviours being socialized in a particular culture.

Taking the view of a person who expects the ombudsman to fill the roles of *ally* and *instrument*, I shall explore nationally distinct narratives. I do this by creating archetype German and British characters that are an amalgamation of the two roles in the dataset in the two countries. These characters are grounded in the data but are ideal types created for the purpose of adding analytic value. The characters are equipped with a good dose of common sense, as well as being politically aware and engaged citizens.

A German Complainant

As explained in Chapter 2, a *typical German* grows up amongst many rules and endless efficiency. Deeply significant to the German legal and political culture is the *Grundgesetz* (basic law) from 1949. It put Germany on a path to a strong and stable constitutional democracy, clearly distancing itself from its past. Arguably, this has enhanced the role of basic rights and their prominence in the German legal order—unlike in Britain (Lazarus 2004: 24). Basic rights are viewed as a 'system of values' or 'objective norms' which radiate throughout the whole legal system (Alexy 1990). Here we must be careful not to assume that rights carry the same significance across different legal traditions, cultures and languages (Lazarus 2004: 24). Rights have a specific 'social and historical substance' (Puchalska-Tych and Salter 1996). Guided by a strong and stable set of entrenched basic rights, our German complainant has shaped her view about legality, fairness, justice and legitimacy. The relationship to authority is thus one defined by a strong sense of legality and order. The following provides examples from the data that underline this notion, taking the shape of a German complainant, one who complains to the insurance ombudsman and another who complains to the SÖP. Both characters show similar expectations towards the ombudsman.

Expectations of a person who turns to the insurance ombudsman:

> I expect the ombudsman to enforce my goals and that the unreasonable rejection by my insurance company is punished. It went completely against my sense of legality. I want the ombudsman to put things right and help me to enforce my rights in a cost-free and fast procedure. I further want to know if my claim is within the law and if I am right or if I am wrong. The ombudsman needs to investigate the legality of the insurance company. I need a clear statement whether my claim is legally feasible and I need an objective assessment of the situation.

Using very similar terms, a person who turns to the transport ombudsman expects:

> I want to overcome my powerlessness towards the airline. On top of that, approaching a lawyer or using the Internet portal of the airline would have cost me a good 20% of the value of the dispute. I wanted the SÖP as a competent, powerful and free advocate, ally and intermediary. I consider it a scandal that lawyers and Internet portals can easily make so much money off the griev-

> ances of travellers. I also don't want to have to get a lawyer. My experience has taught me that a letter from a lawyer can move a lot. This is, unfortunately, a symptom of our times, even if the consumer has the law on her side, nothing happens without a lawyer. I expect a conciliation offer to be made, based on the case law. I wanted a legal clarification of my case without having to consult my legal protection insurance. Based on previous good experience with Lufthansa I didn't want to take them to court but find an acceptable solution. Bottom line, I want my rights to be recognized and to get a refund from the airline.

These examples of expectations towards the ombudsman—drawn from *ally* and *instrument* characterizations in the dataset—demonstrate how a German complainant typically uses very legalistic terms when communicating with and about an ombudsman. Apart from the difference in context and content of the individual complaint to the insurance ombudsman and to the transport ombudsman, it is evident that the same kind of language of legality is used. Here an interesting phenomenon can be observed. It appears that the ombudsman have been set up in line with the German national legal culture, which is heavily focused on rights, hierarchy and authority. In many ways the ombudsman replicate the formal justice system. As mentioned before, the institutional set-up of an ombudsman has typically one ombudsman (retired judge) at the top of the hierarchy, assisted by qualified lawyers dealing with complaints. As a result, the informal ombudsman process is turned into a formalistic and hierarchical institution, closely aligned to the law. This might not fill the aim and purpose of informal justice criteria, but it nurtures the German national legal socialization. What do I mean by this? If we assume that our German complainant is unaware of the full purpose and meaning of an ombudsman and then encounters a familiar structure, she will be more likely to be able to formulate her expectations informed by her socialization with the formal legal system. I argue further that, even if the ombudsman cannot fulfil these criteria, our complainant will enter the ombudsman process crediting the authority of the ombudsman with legitimacy and trust because of who they are (judges and lawyers) rather than because it is an ADR process. As noted above, trust and legitimacy can easily be broken down through context-specific perceptions of procedural justice, for example. However, reading from the data, it is evident that our German complainant who expects the ombudsman to be an *ally* and *instrument* has a clear instinct about this type of dispute resolution as being a legalistic and familiar one, based on the hierarchical court structure.

A British Complainant

A *typical British* complainant, socialized by the national legal culture described in Chapter 2, grows up without a set of values enshrined in a constitution. The lack of codifying values in law means, amongst other things, that legal patriotism in Britain coheres around parliamentary sovereignty and the piecemeal development of common law. The British 'prefer simply to set out, in general terms, the non-negotiable components of our identity'.[3] Our British complainant grew up amongst people who tend to grumble about the state of things rather than actively complaining about them. In common parlance, Britain does not have a state but a government and (despite its centralized political system) people exhibit a strong attachment to the local. Policy is decentralized and a matter for the people, not remote politicians. Further, as Koch (2016: 3) notes, 'there is little doubt that growing numbers of citizens are disenchanted with formal politics in Great Britain'. This results in a trend of little faith in political leaders and institutions and, as a consequence, a loss of trust that the government serves people's interest (Power Inquiry 2007; Denver et al. 2012). Taking an anthropological view of the typical English, Fox (2014: 2) observes that 'the principal effect of globalization … has been an increase in nationalism and tribalism, a proliferation of struggles for independence, devolution and self-determination and a refulgence of concern about ethnicity and cultural identity in almost all parts of the world, the UK is no exception'.

Similar to the German complainant, I offer an amalgamated British complainant born out of the dataset, expecting the ombudsman to be an *ally* and *instrument*. Our British complainant is of similar nature as her German counter-part: she has shaped her view about legality, fairness, justice and legitimacy in her national context. The relationship to authority, in contrast to our German complainant, is defined by a mixture of distrust in politics and government, accompanied by high expectations, even a feeling of entitlement, towards public services. Representative examples from the dataset are provided, merged into one complainant to the FOS and one to the energy ombudsman.

A person who approaches OS: Energy would expect:

> I want the ombudsman to act on my (the consumer's) behalf. Hopefully with some 'teeth' or power behind them, to force the Energy Provider to finally do what ANY self-respecting company trading within the UK should do, i.e. treat its customers with SOME level of service and respect. I expect the ombudsman

[3]http://www.telegraph.co.uk/comment/telegraph-view/3618632/Ten-core-values-of-the-British-identity.html.

> to force the energy provider to do something reasonable, i.e. arrange for future billing to be adjusted in line with usage, make refunds for previous overbilling, and provide compensation. The energy supplier needs to be brought to justice and the problem needs sorting to my satisfaction. The ombudsman needs to force the energy supplier to sort out my bills accurately and make them talk with each other as nobody was taking responsibility for dealing with my complaint. I expect the ombudsman to sanction the energy supplier for such a serious failure and to push for a payment that closer matches the amount of time that I have spent investigating. I expect a financial gesture of goodwill to compensate for my time and cost involved in dealing with this issue.

Similar to the above complainant, a person who contacts FOS would say:

> I expected the FOS to review my case and request the insurer to honour the agreement and pay me the insurance they owed me. I also expected the ombudsman to enquire into the matter and to oblige the management company to make the fair offer it had undertaken to make and increase the compensation offered to cover the fall in annuity rates. This seemed to me to be the only fair solution since the management company was saying that this was covered in their offer although they had, in fact, ignored it and included nothing for it. The ombudsman should make an unbiased decision as to whether this was an ethical decision by the Bank to be fair and consider the circumstances. The ombudsman needs to take my human rights on board and liaise with me rather than paperwork from the banks, which does not reflect the conversations they had with me. I wrote to the Ombudsman to seek reinstatement of the mortgage and drawdown facility. I expected that they would investigate, conclude that the bank had no right to withdraw the facility. As a secondary position, I anticipated that they would say that if there was any right to do so it could only be done with prior notice (in which case I could have withdrawn the overpayment so I could continue to access it in need). I believed that the Ombudsman had authority to force the bank to what it says (though I have learnt since it does not).

Narratives around fairness and justice, similar to her German counterpart, display a complainant who is knowledgeable and has fairly clear expectations of the process. Whether these expectations are justified and reasonable or not is another matter. The data revels that the British complainant does not frame the expectations around legality and uses much less formal language compared to the German complainant. The narratives tend to be focused on being heard and getting an apology. How does this match with the national legal culture and socialization? Unlike in Germany, the British don't have a distinct relationship to legal order and hierarchy. The courts are not seen as an efficient dispute resolution model for consumer complaints. They are overrun and have unpredictable outcomes, duration and costs. Also, typically, consumers do not take their complaints to a court (Gill et al. 2017), but mostly do nothing and remain disgruntled, thus losing trust in the justice system (European Social Survey (ESS) Chapter 2). Similarly in Germany, the numbers of people going to court is decreasing (Höland and Meller-Hannich 2017). Berlin (2014) finds that people mainly go to court in Germany when the value of the complaint is high (p. 53). This means that the courts are not viewed as a sensible option for consumer redress. With this background, our British consumer approaches the ombudsman with an existing notion of cynicism towards the formal system. Interestingly, the ombudsmen in the UK are set up very differently from their German equivalents. In contrast to the German version, I believe that the ombudsman model in the UK is set up as a counter-balance to the formality and inaccessibility of the courts. As a result, the UK ombudsmen provide a less formal and less legalistic process than their German counterparts, in comparison to the distinct German approach and attitude towards the formal system. In the UK national system, the architecture of the less legalistic approach to ADR is designed to enhance legitimacy, trust and acceptance.

To conclude, our German complainant is motivated by legalistic, formalistic and hierarchical attitudes when approaching the ombudsman. In contrast, seeking justice, an explanation and an apology motivates our British complainant. Both seeking redress for their complaint, possibly even expecting the same outcome, approach the ombudsman process with contrasting attitudes. These attitudes reflect a national socialization that influences our notions of fairness, justice and how we relate to authorities. The data also infers that our British and our German complainants will have different sets of expectations of the ombudsman. Chapter 7 will go on to show what this signifies for wider considerations about social meanings of ombudsman and where complainants place ombudsman/ADR in the justice system.

The examination of the data in this chapter has revealed a shared demographic, besides distinct national patterns of expectations of ombudsman. A typical respondent to the survey (across the entire dataset) was male over 50 years old, educated and employed (Creutzfeldt 2016c). Looking at ombudsman annual reports, the same pattern emerges throughout the ombudsman in my study, with slight differences between the UK public and private sectors.[4] This opens up another set of questions as to why people who could arguably easily navigate the formal justice system are typical users of the informal system.

[4]The dataset for the public sector ombudsmen showed a broader variation of users.

Conclusions

This chapter set out to contribute to a better understanding of how people form their attitudes towards an ombudsman. I explored these attitudes through the qualitative empirical dataset of responses of recent ombudsman users in Germany and the UK. This inquiry was based on the theoretical considerations of legal consciousness and sought to develop a more refined image of people's attitudes and expectations of an ombudsman process. The data revealed four roles that relate to both the full dataset, as well as providing a nationally refined narrative. Based on the national narratives, I argued that people's attitudes towards what is fair, just and legitimate is based on their legal socialization. In other words, people's relationship with law plays a crucial part in how they negotiate their way through, and engage with, the informal system.

The national narratives have shown—expressed through representative voices of two data-constructed complainants, one German and one British—how closely entwined are people's attitudes towards the law with expectations of the informal ombudsman process. This raises a central question about the construction of ideas about justice, legitimacy and trust in the context of informal dispute resolution. What does this mean for the development of informal justice in the national context and in the European context?

Part III

The Future of Informal Justice Systems

7

A European Informal Justice System?

Introduction

How do we construct ideas of justice in alternative dispute resolution (ADR) and online dispute resolution (ODR)? The two empirical Chapters 5 and 6 provided support for the initial assumption that people who are unaccustomed to ADR do not know what to expect from the process. How do people then form their expectations and assumptions about the informal justice system? In Chapter 4 the importance of procedural justice was explored across settings and countries. The data revealed that procedural justice is important to all sampled users, yet also exposed nationally distinct patterns. Taking these findings and adding the lens of legal consciousness and legal socialization to the qualitative data, Chapter 6 considered in more detail the role of a national dimension of expectations of a justice system. I have argued that people rely on what they already know and are familiar with when confronted with a new system. Lacking familiarity with the informal dispute resolution system, people seem to transfer the values, expectations, and attitudes from one system (formal) to another (informal). What does this mean for a European approach to dispute resolution?

A European Approach to Dispute Resolution

I'd argue that there is no such thing as a shared understanding of a European dispute resolution space, nor a functioning and visible system of informal justice. What does exist is a collection of informal mechanisms that offer

N. Creutzfeldt, *Ombudsmen and ADR*, Palgrave Socio-Legal Studies,
https://doi.org/10.1007/978-3-319-78807-4_7

ADR. Existing ADR providers offer their users different standards of procedures. This begs the question if such a thing like a *European identity* for a dispute resolution mechanism is at all achievable or desirable.

A system providing dispute resolution needs to aim to provide justice in their procedures and outcomes. Now, if justice is tied to national cultures and thereby linked to normative assumptions about what is right or wrong or what is fair and unfair, how can this be Europeanized? If what is perceived as just and fair is closely tied to the national context and understanding of social norms, I suggest it is a better strategy to foster a model of ADR that ideally complies with the principles of justice and fairness within the national context. I shall demonstrate what I mean by this in linking the discussion about justice and building ADR to European integration theories. These are neo-functionalism and intergovernmentalism.

The theory of neo-functionalism, rooted in the 1950s, is an integration theory to encourage free trade in a borderless community of countries. Closely aligned with the ideas of the founders of the European Union, Western Europe was subject to this integration. Neo-functionalism is a strategy that promotes the development of shared identities and reduces the exclusionary commitment to nation states (Herrmann et al. 2004: 1). The idea was to encourage cross-state cooperation on a series of functional matters by aiming integration initially at individual sectors with the hope that it would spread to others. In other words, neo-functionalism takes the functionalist principles and applies them to regional institutions. For example, in regulated sectors (energy, telecoms, financial services) the goal was to create shared identities. Ultimately, aiming to create a supranational state, neo-functionalism at its peak sees the nation state decline (Haas 1961; Wieder and Diez 2004; Rosamond 2000).

Intergovernmentalism, also a theory of European integration, supports the notion that national governments control the level and speed of European integration (Moravcsik 1993; Keohane 1991). It thereby challenges the neo-functionalist approach. In other words, supranational organizations do not have the same influence as national governments in driving the integration process. With the idea of integration as a choice, the state-centric intergovernmentalist approach can be understood as a decision-making method. Whilst clinging onto the notion that the state holds control over the direction of integration, domestic interests are held highly. Putting national interests first pertaining to the implementation of laws, for example, could be seen as a result of states failing to assert their interests in the decision-making process (Falkner et al. 2004).

I will use the general aspirations of these two theories to get to the heart of the challenges that ADR faces in Europe. Looking through the neo-functionalist lens at ADR we could understand networks that were set up in support of shared identities and with a commitment to the European project. Guided by European values the EC set up the Financial Dispute Resolution Network (FIN-NET) and Travel-NET, while the National Energy Ombudsman Network (NEON) is set up as an international non-for profit association under Belgian law. These networks provide ADR in member states and are aiming to promote cooperation among national ombudsman and ADR in their specialist sectors. Their aim is also to provide consumers with easy access to ADR in cross-border disputes. EU-wide regulated sectors have been subject to closer scrutiny than other sectors. These sector-specific pan-European networks offer an opportunity for the envisaged spill-over effect, as hoped for by the neo-functionalist approach. This spill-over translates into ADR networks learning and exchanging about best practice, quality control, and key performance indicators, for example. The networks are made up of member states' representatives of the ADR providers or ombudsman and—similar to EU institutions—there remain differences and disagreements about specific national level practices.

Translating the intergovernmentalist approach to ADR in Europe means that national governments will determine the speed of the development of ADR, influenced by their political agendas. Now, this comparison is a bit of a stretch as ADR is not a priority on the national agenda (nor is European integration). If we assume it is for now, then I would support the notion that national actors, leading the integration, play a central role in promoting ADR within their national context to then integrate it into a European space. For ADR to be accepted into the national dispute resolution structure it needs to be seen to provide fair and just procedures. This, I argue, is most likely to be achieved within a national context.

Exploring the consciousness around alternatives to formal legality, then, starts with legality and how this constructs ideas about justice. Our sense of legality contributes, amongst other things, to how we believe a dispute ought to be resolved. In the words of Katsh et al. (1999: 706): 'Every dispute arises in a setting or context, and the setting from which it arises may shape the expectations of the parties, the timing of settlement, the perceived urgency of resolution, the consequences of and available alternatives to failure.'

ADR—considered as an alternative to formal legalistic modes of dispute resolution—has, in recent decades, been encouraged throughout the EU as a means to offer accessible justice. The EU promotes well-functioning ADR to:

> … encourage consumers to seek solutions to the problems they encounter when buying products and services in the Single Market … All EU consumers are entitled to equal access to consumer redress. Therefore quality ADR entities should be available for all types of consumer disputes in all EU Member States. Consumers and traders should also be aware of such opportunities.[1]

As Cortes (2016: 18) argues, the institutional promotion of consumer ADR mechanisms is 'not simply to enable individual redress, but to secure more effective compliance with and enforcement of consumer law which ultimately seek to increase consumer trust in the market' (see also European Commission 2011, 2012).

The type of ODR I describe here goes beyond the ODR platform (Chapter 1) that the EU introduced in 2016 (which is more of a hub for online disputes that connects the complainant with the appropriate national ADR body to handle their complaint). The form of ODR I will be discussing in this chapter is a parallel (to its offline providers) form of dispute resolution with its own processes and outcomes. These are mainly directed by technology and open up the informal dispute resolution space.

With the recent ADR and ODR legislation, European lawmakers intended both to strengthen existing national models of dispute resolution while at the same time overcoming the notion of nationally restricted dispute resolution. The legislation (on paper) offers European consumers an accessible, transparent, coherent and high quality dispute resolution system to improve access to justice—complementing existing national pathways to justice. We can understand this legislation as the EU creating a layer of (informal) justice for its member states. This raises questions not only about the level of engagement of the EU in national matters, but also about what ADR is and means in this context. How can this model of justice be meaningful and accepted throughout the EU if it is defined by its national implementation? Is ADR a form of justice, a process or an outcome? What does access to justice mean in the ADR context? How do providers of ADR see their role and what do users experience as justice? What does ODR, as a system of justice, provide?

[1]Alternative Dispute Resolution and Online Dispute Resolution for EU consumers: Questions and Answers. Accessed on 18 November 2017. http://europa.eu/rapid/press-release_MEMO-12-994_en.htm.

This chapter is structured around these questions in three parts, to help unpack the notion of a European informal justice system. First, the role of the EU in the creation of the informal justice system is outlined. Second, I examine and reflect upon the form of justice that ADR and ODR provide. Third, the concept of access to justice is revisited in the context of ADR and ODR.

The Role of the EU in Creating an Informal Justice System

Law and legal orders operate within a defined jurisdictional frame which is often a geographical space (but not always; for example, it could a national law that is applied extraterritorially). Different spaces have different laws, which means that European law, national law, and formal and informal law can overlap. There are also sector-specific laws that can supersede national laws. In short, a complex web of rules creates a blurring of different systems and spaces of justice. The EU's role in national law is a topic of much debate (Kohler-Koch 2003). The EU attempts to enhance integration through law with a mixture of regulations, directives, and soft law measures that have to be transposed into national laws (Jacobson 2004; Trubek and Trubek 2005). With the aim of regulating and facilitating consumption in the internal market and to protect consumers, European legislators have seen fit to implement legislation on ADR and ODR. At the same time, the internet and e-commerce have opened up a further space in which consumers' rights need protection. The EU has therefore created a pan-European platform that offers ODR.

Challenged by its intrinsic diversity, the EU has shaped the ADR legislation to its member states as a directive. The directive is a legal act that requires member states to achieve a clear result without dictating the measures to be using in achieving that result. In other words, directives are not directly applicable at the national level, but have to be incorporated into national law first. According to article 288 (ex Art 249 TEC) of the Treaty on the Functioning of the EU (TFEU), 'a directive shall be binding as to the result to be achieved, upon each Member State to which it is addressed, but shall leave to the national authorities the choice of form and methods'.[2]

[2]TFEU. Accessed 15 November 2017. http://eur-lex.europa.eu/legal-content/EN/TXT/HTML/?uri=CELEX:12012E288&from=EN.

This has translated into member states implementing the ADR directive with differing commitment into national law (Creutzfeldt 2016b). Some member states have decided to have one ADR body per sector and a clear point of contact for consumers that signposts to the most suitable ADR provider. Other member states have a multitude of ADR providers that might even overlap in their remits with, for example, no clear guidance or signposting alongside. As a result there is no uniformity of quality assurance, availability, or access to ADR bodies across the EU. The varying level of implementation of ADR into the national legal space has already caused many problems.

In the UK, for example, a market for ADR and dispute resolution has opened up where different providers compete for business both within their own country and across borders. In a (to date) non-regulated space, some ombudsman/ADR providers have seized the opportunity to push for a competitive market. Such ADR providers approach businesses and offer lower case fees than their competitor providers to encourage businesses to sign up with them. This might signify unpredictable quality and exacerbate consumer confusion. Furthermore, some companies are acting as intermediaries between the consumer and the ADR provider, offering the consumer a platform (after harvesting their personal data) which then contacts the business directly. Despite competition being a good thing for a market, in this case I believe it could serve to promote a race to the bottom regarding quality and provision of dispute resolution. In addition, it does not contribute to building a visible and easily navigable ADR system. There is currently no requirement for just one ADR body per sector and this can create consumer confusion if the bodies are not properly signposted or notified to the European Commission. A further problem also arises here—that of forum-shopping. This means that an informed consumer can choose to bring their complaint to a specific ADR body from which they expect a favourable outcome. Finally, on top of all these options, the courts can also be called upon.

Another important aspect to consider in this period of ADR expansion is maintaining quality while at the same time providing consistent outcomes. At the moment it is possible to get different outcomes for a similar complaint from different ombudsmen within the same ADR body—needless to say a comparison across sectors is not possible. This might suggest a need for streamlined training for staff of ADR bodies, thus resulting in outcomes that are somewhat more predictable.

Whilst one could argue that a competitive market is a good thing in the pursuit of raising quality standards, it is likely to be a substantial challenge for the user. It adds to the confusion about where to turn to when a consumer has a dispute with a service-provider, for example. In particular, when introducing a new dispute resolution system it needs to be easily accessible, straightforward to navigate, and provide a process that is satisfying. At the time of writing, it is safe to say that the desired access to justice and the hoped for uptake of ADR is yet to materialize.

I offer two possible explanations for the absence of a wave of ADR flooding the EU and washing access to justice over its member states. First, it is not uncommon for EU legislation to have a bumpy national implementation and a delayed effect (Beek 2007; Kaeding and Voskamp 2011). With respect to the national diversity into which the new laws have to be integrated, it was always going to be a challenge. In the process of drafting the ADR directive, which had to meet the approval of all the participating member states, a lot of the initially intended high quality standards and other recommendations got lost along the way.[3] This was the only way to accommodate a workable compromise for all member states and so enable the passing of the legislation. As a result, a directive outlining minimum quality criteria for ADR entities leaves member states with too much leeway with regard to national implementation.

Second, implementation into diverse legal spaces is aligned to culturally specific relationships within the national legal system and exposure to ADR. Some member states have an existing and developed ADR culture, while for example in others it is an unfamiliar (and consequently less trusted) approach. The existing ADR landscape in the member states at the point of national implementation have therefore been very varied and patchy. This has meant that although some member states were ready to embrace the ADR directive and easily integrated it into national legislation, for others it created much more of a challenge (Creutzfeldt 2016b).

The ADR directive was also seen by member states without little or no tradition of ADR as an incentive to improve their dispute resolution systems. Some countries, in creating ADR bodies, based them on well-established existing models. For example, in Germany the *Versicherungsombudsmann* was used as a template for the creation of other ADR at a national level. Similarly, the Financial Ombudsman Service in the UK, as the largest provider of ADR, has been taken as a template for

[3]For example, the ADR directive leaves leeway to have an ADR body within a business provoking the question of impartiality. In this instance, France was a driving force for maintaining this option as it has a long-standing history of in-house *mediateurs*.

other countries' ADR bodies. However, this raises questions about whether a model that has been developed to serve a specific sector is transferable to function in other contexts.

Currently, the EU's ambitions to create full ADR coverage have not been met. There are not enough ADR bodies with clear competencies in the member states. The ADR directive required member states to set up residual bodies that would deal with all those complaints that existing specialised ADR providers were not covering. This not only adds to the confusion of where to turn, but also directly affects the success of the ODR platform. The ODR regulation required a platform, or portal, to be established. The idea is to have one online gateway or point of entry to help find the right ADR body in the right member state to help with complaints about e-commerce. The portal is hosted by the EC and operated in all the official European languages.[4] Despite the portal having been in operation since early 2016, it can only perform its function if there are enough registered national ADR providers. This is not yet the case and so the portal is having some teething problems. This, in turn, will affect people who have already reached out for help from the platform only to remain dissatisfied.

What about the users of all these interconnected systems? How are the systems negotiated and how do we make sense of them in our everyday lives? It is fair to say that most people are likely to have very little precise knowledge about the functioning of the justice system itself, let alone ADR. For example, throughout our daily lives we encounter a variety of rules and regulations without even being aware of it. They become part of our routines, like stopping at traffic lights, obtaining parking tickets, and entering into consumer contracts when purchasing, for example, goods and services or wi-fi and software agreements that nobody reads but which have legal effects. Indeed, we only have to actively engage with the justice system if something goes wrong. At that point, I argue, we have to consider the power of legality and legal socialization in shaping a popular understanding of justice. To make things even more complicated, these conceptions mean different things to different people within a diverse EU.

Nor is there enough awareness of ADR in most member states, resulting in a much lower uptake than anticipated (assuming, here, that people would use ADR if they knew about it). This has had a direct effect upon develop-

[4]The scope of the ODR legislation also includes business-to-consumer (b2-c) disputes, unlike the ADR directive that deals only with consumer-to-business (c2b) disputes. The platform has four steps to resolve a dispute: (1) submission of complaint online; (2) agreement on ADR entity; (3) case-handling by ADR entity; and (4) outcome and closure.

ing trust in the new arrangements because it is not immediately apparent that it is united system. I believe that the unconnected way in which member states have implemented the ADR directive into their national laws has led to further confusion, as opposed to an increase in access to justice.

Hand in hand with the efforts to create a European space and a system of informal justice, the phenomena of localization has grown (Amin and Thrift 1995; Wilk 1995; Geddes 2000). Localization is a refocusing towards a national or local identity, national culture, and a rooted sense of belonging. This development is driven by a variety of complex reasons. Taking the context of dispute resolution, for example, our sense of fairness and justice has (typically) been developed throughout our formative years within our community or society. This will be the fall-back position that we rely on when having to make choices about accessing justice and dispute resolution. Might there be parallels with the idea of finding refuge in what we already know and consequently using this knowledge as a reference point when engaging with a new system, rather than enthusiastically embracing the new?

Strassoldo (1992: 46) argued that: 'The New Localism is the search for a refuge from the unsettling confusion of the larger world.' I believe that this sentiment applies to the unknown elements of the ADR process. Lost in the Europeanization of ADR and without a clear understanding of what it actually entails, we draw upon a backdrop of local values and local identity as security from the unknown. Individuals seek to orient themselves in the global space through identifying with a particular culture (Beyer 1992: 62). The emphasis on an own culture is not orientated against another real culture—even if groups who are concerned often underline this factor—but against feared effects of processes of globalization (Schuerkens 2003: 217).

Taking a step back from European legislators' ambitions to increase confidence in purchasing goods and services in the single market by providing ADR and ODR, the next part will move on to examine what form informal justice takes here.

ADR and ODR as a Form of Informal Justice

Justice is considered here, in its broadest sense, from a philosophical and interdisciplinary perspective as a blend of fairness (Rawls 1999), equality and moral correctness (Wrbka 2014: 6), as value-oriented justice that goes beyond legal concepts and touches upon sociological, political, or philosophical ideas (Cotterrell 2005; Bingham 2011). Perhaps it is conceivable to say that our sense of justice is a large contributing factor when negotiating how categories of law intersect with our daily lives. Images of law, and what we believe law is supposed to do for us, are understood through the prism of justice. This is where things get fuzzy: justice is likely to be perceived to have different meanings for different actors navigating the system, and thus provide for a variety of different expectations from it. For example, the law in itself consists of a complex collection of meanings and categories understood differently by people, depending on their experience with and knowledge of the law. The law will look and be understood differently by judges, other members of the legal profession, legal academics, welfare recipients, and vulnerable people, for example. Laws within a system of justice are subject to the constantly changing demands and expectations of the system and thus need to remain adaptable to its users' needs.

In what follows I will explore the development and different understanding of ADR and ODR.[5] Generally speaking, both ADR and ODR are movements born out of a need to increase access to justice and make access to justice catch up with the developments of our times.

Remember, then that here I am focusing on the consumer context. I believe that formal justice, such as a court procedure, is important and necessary for certain types of disputes. Other types of disputes are better placed outside of courts.[6] A lengthy, costly and unpredictable court process is no longer feasible in a society that seeks quick fixes, engages in e-commerce, expects instant responses, forms sharing economies and can use social media to take split-second decisions. Both ADR and ODR have evolved to meet those needs in different ways. A companion of reducing costs and making dispute resolution procedures more accessible, faster, and more predictable is to reduce human interaction and contact. Whilst this has reached its apex in ODR, the ADR process remains a predominantly human-administered procedure with technology acting as an assistant. A clear shift towards resolving a dispute, then, is no longer about humans gathered together in a room, interacting face-to-face, or even talking on the phone. The form and medium of providing justice has changed.

Ombudsmen are currently designed to fit their national dispute resolution context. This translates into a structure that, in many ways, is artificial

[5]Here, I would like to draw attention to a development occurring in parallel with ADR. It concerns a rapidly emerging and changing form of online justice: ODR. To be clear, I am not referring to the EU ODR platform, which is intended to function as a distribution portal for signposting existing ADR bodies. The ODR platform referred to here does not resolve disputes.

[6]I am also not talking here about court-annexed meditation, or other forms of ADR that typically happen in person (face-to-face).

as it serves the type of people that created it and overlooks others. It is not a system that provides access to ADR for all, but rather for a selected few. These few, according to my research, are the same people who are able to easily navigate the formal justice system (Creutzfeldt 2016c). For the majority of consumers ADR remains invisible and inaccessible.[7] The lack of clear information and signposting of ADR, along with the fact that people are usually fed up and disgruntled already after complaining to the company or public body, are obstacles to the path to redress. Another contributing factor, once an ombudsman is located, might be the procedures that ombudsmen offer. Most ombudsmen are using 1960s technology and approaches to solve twenty-first-century problems.

Online Dispute Resolution: Digital, On-demand Justice in Cyberspace

The internet provides an endless space that remains largely unregulated (Schwartz 2005; Marsden 2011). Alongside expanding opportunities, the internet also brings many problems with it; one of which is how to properly *do* dispute resolution in cyberspace. Matching its medium, ODR as a dispute resolution model favours technology over people and algorithms over communication. What is ODR? I would suggest that we understand it as a tool that enables access to a certain form of dispute resolution.

If we might question the 'justice part' that ODR delivers, what about the fairness part? For example, Wells (2008) has considered perceptions of fairness where there has been no human interaction at all and found that people caught speeding by automated camera systems often experienced the process as unfair and unjust. She argues that while:

> [The] techno-fix is guaranteed to be fair in one sense [since it is always 'right'] … a machine is unable to demonstrate respect, respond politely or provide the ears necessary for an individual to feel that their voice has been heard. [T]hese additional criteria implicitly necessitate the involvement of human beings in procedurally just encounters (801).

[7] The scope of this volume does not allow to go into this point in more detail, however, with Chris Gill, I will be looking at this particular issue in a new project on Access to Justice, Alternative Dispute Resolution, and consumer Vulnerability in the European Energy Sector (2017–2020): ESRC grant reference ES/P010237/1. See https://esrcjustenergy.wordpress.com.

How can procedural justice, ethical standards and reliable quality be assured online if it is already proving a challenge offline? Also, how can our expectations about what ODR can reasonably offer us be managed? Can we talk about *justice* in this context, or is it something else, perhaps an emotion, that is triggered through ODR (a feeling of relief that it's over)? I suggest that a starting point for this discussion is to be clear what we mean when we speak about ODR, by considering what ODR is being compared with. If we are comparing ODR to the type of dispute resolution that a court, court-annexed mediation, or other form of ADR produces, then we might be looking in the wrong place. The type of dispute resolution ODR offers is far removed from the origins of ADR and its methods or tools of settling disputes. It has rid itself of the personal—the human dimensions of communication, interaction, face-to-face communication, compromise, apologizing and repairing relationships (Ury et al. 1988; Sander and Goldberg 1994; Fisher and Ury 2012; Goldberg et al. 2012: 1–13).

Then we have to think about exclusion: ODR does not provide access for those who are not computer literate or not able to navigate the internet. Through those who do not use the internet would arguably not purchase an item online. Nevertheless, ODR is continuing to take on different forms and this opens the question about how to regulate a space without borders.

One example of a regulated ODR space is that of the online courts in the UK. The concept of online courts was introduced in England and Wales in February 2015 by an advisory group of the Civil Justice Council (2015). The aim is to revolutionize the way in which low-value civil claims are handled, namely through ODR. A new internet-based court system, 'HM Online Court', decides cases on an online basis, corresponding electronically with the parties. Early resolution can be brought about through facilitators. The main incentive for setting up this online court is to enhance access to justice and to help the court system save a lot of money. Although strongly supported by the government and senior judiciary, it is a controversial development. Prominent representatives of the legal profession and advice sector have expressed doubts about the viability and suitability of ODR and its potential impact on access to justice and the 'digitally excluded' (Unlock the Law 2015; Bindman 2017).[8] Is dispute resolution a matter of proportionality? Scholars have argued for appropriate dispute resolution in different contexts (see Menkel-Meadow 2014). Generally speaking,

[8]See also 'The case for online courts' at UCL Judicial Institute, London, 17 February 2017. https://www.laws.ucl.ac.uk/event/the-case-for-online-courts/.

the aim of proportionate dispute resolution is to ensure that the means and cost of resolving disputes is proportionate to the importance and nature of the issues at stake (Elliott and Thomas 2012: 299). However, we can argue about the fact that the importance and nature of the issues at stake might not always be easy to determine. Following the logic of proportionality then, how can we determine its applicability in an ODR context? According to Lord Neuberger:

> There may well be a risk that ODR will lead to more imperfect justice than traditional systems of resolving disputes in court, but I am firmly of the view that the resolution of disputes provided by the state should be proportionate to the issues involved.

In their recent book *Digital Justice*, Katsh and Rabinovich-Einy (2017) outline how the internet produces conflicts and critically examine how technology can be exploited to prevent, resolve and also produce such conflict. The book sheds light upon the next generation of access to justice and how the digital future has no space for courthouses. Is this an upgrade of justice, or possibly an inevitable development, in its own right, that we need to embrace and get to grips with it? The authors state that 'improving access to justice has been an ongoing process, and on-demand justice should be a natural part of our increasingly on-demand society'. Further, any contribution to the debate on improving access to justice includes the need for proposing new dispute resolution processes and new ways to avoid disputes.

Katch and Rabinovich-Einy (2017: 3) state that 'digital justice is about the role of the law and the processes that are emerging to enable individuals to resolve disputes.' ODR is 'a shift from human intervention to one assisted by software' (2017: 47). Justice here is understood in a procedural sense, in the same way as it has appeared in the access to justice literature. I suggest that we need to have a discussion about the emerging trends in the online space and to think about what models (of justice) are developing and how we can regulate them. Are we steering towards a model of predictable justice through algorithms (Paris Innovation Review 2017)? Susskind and Susskind (2015) make a case for algorithms and their capacity to handle a very large number of disputes and thereby potentially provide access to justice in 'numbers never before possible'. If we treat an algorithm as a procedure, a formula, or a tool for making a decision, it has to be crafted and taught to do its job. Moving away from human and individualized justice, algorithms can be applied, can be intelligent and learn, can predict behaviour, and be improved. The possibilities seem endless. At the outset of this process there is, however, a human who programs algorithms. This means that biases can be introduced into the system (that can have an effect on the fairness of the process). Does this create a compromise between efficiency and fairness? Rabinovich-Einy (2006) argues that appropriate design and legal choices in ODR can help reduce cognitive bias in both parties and human disputes resolvers, and this also improves the ability to reach high-quality outcomes.

What does the development of ODR mean for the offerings of informal dispute resolution systems? Is the menu getting too large to choose from? Has the time come to be more precise about defining specific processes for specific types of disputes? And if we do this, what form or type of justice do these processes provide? How much weight does procedural justice—"having one's day in court"—carry in ODR? Is the vanishing trial rhetoric appropriate here or are we witnessing the creation of a new *legal* space? All these important questions will find some form of answer during the evolution of ODR, whilst also raising new ones. I return to the argument I made about ADR earlier. I believe that ODR has great value in helping to sort out disputes that are of small value and that reoccur (e.g. consumer disputes). Such disputes can be dealt with in an online process, delivering fast, accessible, and somewhat predictable outcomes. Having been socialized in a generation that advocated human interaction and communication to solve problems, ideally face-to-face, I am myself habituated towards what I know and feel most comfortable with. But seeing the ease with which the next generation navigates the internet and expects instant reactions, I also appreciate the need for a new, appropriate form of protection of that space.

Access to Informal Justice

The existing difference in language, culture and traditions in Europe pose an added challenge to accessing justice. We are confronted with a web of systems providing dispute resolution. The emergence of the right to effective access to justice has gone hand in hand with the development of social rights (Cappelletti and Garth 1977). As Cappelletti has argued:

> The access-to-justice movement, as a theoretical approach, while certainly rooted in the realistic criticism of formalism and legal dogmatics, tends toward a vision more faithful to the complexity of human society. While the normative component of the law is not denied, it is seen as one element, and quite often not even the principal one of the law. The primary element is the people, with all their cultural, economic and psychological features. Moreover,

the institutions and processes are prominent in this realistic vision. The result of the access-to-justice approach is a 'contextual' conception of the law (Cappelletti 1993: 283).

Access to justice, then, means that we all have the right to be 'treated fairly according to the law and if you are not treated fairly being able to get appropriate redress' (Robins 2011). Access to redress reaches beyond a lawyer and courts. 'It means access to ombudsmen, advice agencies and the police. It means public authorities behaving properly. It means everyone having some basic understanding of his or her rights. It means making law less complex and more intelligible' (Moorhead 2011). What does access to informal justice, as a contextual conception, look like? Is that the form of justice and access that European legislators envisage for ADR and ODR? How is a conception of access to justice different if it becomes an all-inclusive notion—including that of informal justice—to provide redress alongside the formal traditional system of justice?

A starting point to addressing these questions is to consider two positions that form part of this system: the ombudsman and their users. By referring to my qualitative interview data, some understanding is brought to the current debate about law, justice and fairness.

Ombudsman Views: What Does the Law Have to Do with It?

How do the ombudsmen see themselves placed in the informal justice system and what is their relationship with the law? This is interesting not least in relation to public acceptance, trust and use of the ombudsman. The ombudsman system, often described as a hybrid structure (Reif 2013: 395ff), fulfils different functions and has different relationships in and with the law. In other words, the ombudsmen are guided by a variety of rules that place them somewhat at the fringes of the law (Chapter 3).[9]

As part of the elite interviews I conducted for this study, I asked ombudsmen 'What role does the law play in your day-to-day decision-making?' The German insurance ombudsman said: 'Ombudsmen act *within the law* and refer exactly to the legal situation in all their correspondence. If people are not happy with the outcome they are clearly directed to the courts as a next

[9] In particular, the private and organizational ombudsmen that are not established as part of the administrative justice system.

step.' Remember that the ombudsman (ADR) system in Germany is very formal and legalistic, with retired judges as ombudsman and staff that are all qualified lawyers. This means that, although the ombudsmen do not provide binding decisions, they are still representing the law by virtue of their past experience, their training and their letterheads. Here, different ADR providers approach their public profile in different ways, but for the insurance ombudsman, for example, all correspondence is coming directly from *him*.

In the UK, the ombudsmen are set up very differently. Unlike in Germany, there is no clear professional profile of a person working as an ombudsman—there is no need for a legal background or degree. Rather ombudsmen and staff are trained on a need-to-know basis on the applicable legal contexts. Having said that, most ombudsman at the top of an ADR body are qualified lawyers. The response from some UK ombudsman to the question about the role of law in their day-to-day practice is that 'we take the law into consideration to make decisions. However our decisions are based on what is fair and reasonable which makes us more flexible than the law, we have a wider remit than the law.' It is common to have several ombudsmen in one ADR body in the UK, unlike in Germany where there is only one ombudsman at the top of the hierarchy. Another UK ombudsman told me that 'to reach a decision about what a fair outcome you have to *be law savvy*'. It also appeared that the UK ombudsman I interviewed did not feel the need to tell consumers that they are free to take their case to a court if they are not satisfied with the ombudsman' decision—possibly to prevent more complex formal court cases.

Does it matter how the ombudsmen see themselves in relation to the law and how does this impact on their services? Further, this raises question of whether the ombudsman act *with*, *above*, *before*, or *around* the law. First, while the ombudsmen take law, regulation, and legal decisions into account, it is not for them to interpret or determine points of law. Second, a public sector ombudsman may be given the power to initiate its own investigations and private sector ombudsman can identify and feed back systemic failure to the relevant oversight body, regulator, or trade association, recommending investigation and change and thereby influencing policy. Third, the immediacy of digital communications and online service provision is at odds with the delays inherent in lengthy court cases before a decision is reached—although, despite this, people may still want their day in court. Fourth, given the ability of private ombudsman schemes to reach their conclusions relatively rapidly, they enable action to be taken in what is as close as possible to a real-time basis. Finally, analysis of patterns of behaviour across sectors and the conclusions drawn by ombudsman schemes could support additional proactive action by regulatory bodies.

To sum up, the ombudsmen have a clear understanding of where to place themselves and their institution with regard to the law and how flexible they can be in relation to resolving disputes. The described differences range from directly applying the law to determining what is fair and reasonable. As explained to me by the ombudsmen, this can lead to varied possibilities of outcomes. It is possible for two individuals to approach an ombudsman with the same problem and get two different outcomes. Although this shows the flexibility of an ADR process, it also shows the unpredictability and uncertainty of this process. Ordinary people who use the ombudsman system, on the other hand, are not necessarily aware of what the ombudsman can provide for them, what role the law plays in their decision-making, and how this can affect them.

I cannot show a direct causality between the identified ombudsman narratives, how they understand their role, and how their users respond. For this I would need to conduct a longitudinal study over time, for example. What I can do, however, is to provide data on how the users of the ombudsman construct their expectations along different narratives and, after that, I offer a suggestion of how they might be connected.

The User Perspective: Is It Fair?

The data I am drawing upon for this section are the open-ended responses in the survey about users' expectations and explanations of the nature of their complaint to the ombudsman. The ombudsmen, discussed above, have a clear understanding of where to place themselves in relation to the law, even if that understanding varies between interviewees. The users of the ombudsman, on the other hand, mostly uninformed about what the ombudsman can do for them, rely on their common sense and their expectations of what they think is fair, based upon their expectations of the systems of justice they are accustomed to, as seen in Chapter 4.

The narratives of users are built around the clear desire to be treated according to what is fair. However, this raises questions around what fairness means. Does fairness mean the user being put back into the position pre-complaint? Is fairness to be given a voice, even though one might not get the outcome hoped for? Is fairness, perhaps, a form of education and expectations management rather than the achievement of an outcome? Does being treated in a fair and reasonable way mean different things to different complainants?

Building on the desire for procedural justice (Chapter 4 and the narratives described in Chapter 5), expectations of UK ombudsman users are framed around fairness and German ombudsman users frame their expectations around the law. Connecting the expectations of users to the above ombudsman' views, I believe that we witness a reaction towards formal authority as a response to the unknown of ADR. This takes different forms in the countries discussed here. A German ombudsman, a (retired) judge, exerts formality, authority and respect. He/she is closely aligned to the formal legal system even, arguably, still seen to be part of it. The data reveals that a German user would takes a very legalistic approach to the ombudsman and in return expects a highly legal response and, indeed, be more likely to accept it as he/she would treat it as an official, legal decision. Whereas, in contrast, I argue that a UK ombudsman exerts informality (as opposed to the formal features of a court), seeking to solve a complaint according to what is fair and reasonable. The focus is also on the organization of the ombudsman rather than on the individual, as in Germany. Distancing themselves clearly from the formal legal system, UK ombudsman brand themselves as: 'inquisitive', 'listening', 'learning', and seeking to find 'new and improved ways of doing things'. The UK has chosen a more flexible approach to informal justice and I think it is safe to assume that the user, as a reaction to his/her relationship to authority, will be more agreeable to this style of ombudsman as long as they get the outcome they desire. If not, then a sense of 'having a day in court' might then come to the surface (Stipanowich 2004).

Does ADR offer justice and is it the same as fairness? The ombudsmen (as seen above) have different outlooks on the role that the law plays in their daily dealings with complaints. The UK ombudsmen use the law as a guiding framework or a benchmark and rely heavily on what they deem fair and reasonable in the situation. Their German counterparts, in comparison, base their procedures and decisions firmly on the law. Both approaches satisfy the respective market (legal cultures) in which they are situated, or are a product of it. I wonder if this produces a system of ADR that does not ultimately provide justice, as we traditionally understand it, but rather a hybrid form of justice and fairness: an adaptable service to the individual users' needs. These needs are met though sector-specific ombudsman that provide a service designed and refined to address a specific type of complaint. I have come to believe that popular understanding of justice cannot be disentangled from fairness when asking people about their expectations of ombudsmen. Assuming that justice and fairness merge into one construct when thinking about ombudsmen and ADR, the question arises as to whether ombudsman and ADR can shape an identity outside of the shadow of the formal national legal culture.

Matching the user perspective with that of the legislator and that of the ombudsman is a challenge. How can trust and credibility be built into the ADR system? One answer is by producing consistent social justice[10] outcomes for individuals and business. As discussed above, these outcomes vary according to different types of complaints and people's expectations of the procedure (Gilad 2008; Creutzfeldt 2014). How then can this apparent divide be challenged?

In summary, we might ask how much these identified divisions and member states' national specificities restrict the EU's aim to create an informal dispute resolution system that fulfils its purpose in everyday use. I am sceptical that a pan-European approach to ADR is desirable, as I do not think we can treat ADR as a unified model of dispute resolution. I believe it is more productive to think of ADR in context, aiming to produce an accepted and trusted model of 'national' dispute resolution. This is not to say that an ADR model cannot work across national borders. In regulated sectors, such as financial services and energy, for example, there are EU networks and dispute resolution models in place. However, they are also heavily influenced by their national context (Bradford and Creutzfeldt *forthcoming* 2018).

Conclusions

I have outlined in this chapter the challenges to defining a European informal justice system. EU legislators intended to strengthen national models of dispute resolution and overcome the notion of nationally restricted dispute resolution by implementing legislation on ADR and ODR. The motivation here is to increase the purchasing power across borders in the European common market through providing a dispute resolution system. This has not, however, created an identifiable informal justice system. It might be too early to make this claim, as the legislation is relatively young. Yet, the acceptance of ADR into everyday practice is far from visible.

I offered the following four explanations. First, the member states have chosen different levels of implementation of ADR into their national legal

[10]Social justice is generally equated with the notion of equality or equal opportunity in society. It can be seen as access to justice in this context.

space. This means that ADR is placed into existing models of dispute resolution, within the national legal culture. This makes it difficult for a European informal justice system to be meaningful and accepted as such.

Second, and related, is that the way in which people (who responded to my survey) make sense of the ADR bodies is through their existing impressions of the legal system as it shapes their understanding of justice. This, in turn, suggests that ADR (and ODR) as forms of informal justice might have to earn acceptance despite an impediment of no pre-existing clear set of expectations and engagement. As a result, a trend is detected towards a focus on the local and national, moving away from the European and globalized.

Third, a layer of complexity is added through ODR. Having found that people are not accessing the ADR system and are still negotiating its legitimacy, ODR is a further pathway of choice. I posit that we need to be careful what ODR is compared to. It might be best to understand it as a form of ADR that comes with its own set of online procedures and rules, some of which still have to be developed, defined and matured into.

Finally, having portrayed the web of available ADR and ODR providers and processes available for consumers when facing a dispute, it seems less clear how to translate this into an easily accessible, transparent and fast pathway to redress. In the next chapter, I discuss whether ADR needs to generate its own norms of fairness, justice and language from the inside-out.

8

Growing Informal Justice (from the Inside-Out)

Introduction

In Chapter 2, I set out to explore Europe's informal justice systems. Amidst the complex web of national formal legal settings and rules, the informal justice system is understood as 'non-bureaucratic, local, [and] accessible for ordinary people' (Palmer et al. 2005). Although the EU is legislating to create a European informal justice space, at this point in time we do not have one system of informal justice. In this book I have focused on consumer alternative dispute resolution (ADR) in the private sector and have also discussed ombudsmen in the public sector. Private and public ombudsmen perform similar functions in different parts of the justice systems (see Chapter 3). The ombudsman is an example of an established institution providing ADR, informing my deliberations about the informal dispute resolution system more generally. Guided by my empirical evidence, I have argued that an evolving informal justice system is very much to be understood within its national context and, more precisely, through its relationship to the formal legal system. This implies two things when it comes to developing informal justice systems. First, that the European project of creating an informal justice system is premature, as there is no such thing as a shared understanding of a European dispute resolution space, let alone a functioning and visible system of informal justice. It is more productive to think of it as a collection of informal mechanisms. Second, returning to the question of legitimacy

N. Creutzfeldt, *Ombudsmen and ADR*, Palgrave Socio-Legal Studies,
https://doi.org/10.1007/978-3-319-78807-4_8

and trust in developing an informal system and its institutions (ombudsman), I argue that we need to understand, to develop, and to shape ADR in a national context and, only after that, to start to promote its proliferation into the European space. In other words, ADR needs to grow from the inside—out.

I develop this argument in three parts, guided by the query about a productive way to think about what informal justice actually is. With the aim of creating a system that is recognized, trusted and used, I contend that ADR is best able to create its own norms within a national cultural and legal context. In the first part I question if ADR actually has an identity that produces its own norms. The next part develops the argument that ADR has to be understood in its context. We have to recognize a national and local cultural identity and its understanding of dispute resolution. The last part revisits the users of the informal justice system and discusses procedural needs. I conclude with some deliberations about what the future holds.

Out of Law's Shadow: Can ADR Create Its Own Norms?

Currently, it is safe to say that ADR has not lived up to its predicted impact and uptake in EU member states. ADR appears as a hybrid, flexible form of providing redress, without a recognizable identity. This lack of identity can be understood from different angles. The reason for adding ADR to a system of formal justice was to ease access to justice for consumers and to enable a faster, cheaper, and more accessible pathway to redress. Therefore, ADR processes are designed to be flexible and typically less rigid than the formal court-centred system. As O'Brien (2002) puts it: 'if the law is cold and rigid in its adherence to universal principle, an ombudsman is warm and supple in his or her response to the particular'. Whilst this can be a strength in terms of procedures, interactions and outcomes, the flexibility does not contribute to generating a shared ADR (or even ombudsman) identity. The multitude of different approaches that are united under the umbrella of ADR makes it problematic to understand what form of ADR is meant (Doyle et al. 2014). For example, the most common association when talking about ADR, I suggest, is that of mediation. Mediation has become a requirement, for example, in family law matters, before a court can be involved (Hopt and Steffek 2012) and family mediation is usually a court-annexed process (Cantwell 2016; Mair 2017). Importantly, mediation in that context is quite different from the mediation that is offered in an ombudsman procedure or the mediation that is offered in online dispute resolution (ODR). It is evident, then, that we have a system that provides many different pathways to redress in which the terms commonly used do not always share the same meaning.

To measure the uptake, impact, and acceptance of ombudsmen we use concepts that are familiar to us, such as justice, fairness, legitimacy and trust. Different types of ombudsmen serve different sectors and have different functions, but essentially they are part of the large ADR toolkit. In order to assess if such a thing as ADR socialization (identity) exists, or if it is a worthwhile endeavour to strive towards, we need to look at both the national and the European contexts where we find that there are nationally distinct patterns of ADR in each member state. Although there are sector-specific ombudsman that might deal with the same type of complaints in different countries, they are likely to have different procedures to reach the respective outcomes. As I have demonstrated through my data in Chapters 5 and 6, a popular understanding of justice informs people's expectations of ombudsmen and ADR. This, in turn, creates social meanings of ombudsmen and ADR in a national context. ADR is usually added to an existing justice system to fill gaps, yet does not seem to be able to move out of the shadow of the formal system to be seen as a force in its own right. For it to come out of the shadow it needs to develop its own identity. This is in itself a challenge.

Informal justice and ADR are, as mentioned before, not one homogeneous thing. Norrie (1996) argues that we should not think only in terms of state/non-state or formal/informal because the range of types of justice is much more diverse. Here lies the core of the challenge to harmonization; it is a feature of justice—closely related to norms and distinct cultural features—to be understood and built in a local context, so growing ADR from the inside-out might be the best possible option to establish an ADR identity, producing its own norms. This can also include existing public ADR providers sharing the national informal dispute resolution space. Further, might a nationally grown ADR system provide for a richer identity? I am not convinced that the ambition for ADR to become a European-wide dispute resolution system is realistic. The role of the EU in delivering rules for national implementation might be seen as a driver to create norms within the national context. But, ADR is an approach that, by definition, is adaptable, changing and forming according to the demands made of it. I suggest that we turn to the national context when thinking about creating an ADR identity.

Keeping ADR in Context

The objectives of the EU, as set out in the Lisbon Treaty[1] in 2007 (Art 3 of the Treaty on European Union) are (amongst others): the promotion of peace and well-being of EU citizens; an area of freedom, security and justice without internal frontiers; sustainable development based on balanced economic growth and social justice; a social market economy—highly competitive and aiming at full employment and social progress; and a free single market. These ambitions reflect aspirations for a joined yet diverse Europe. Alongside EU legislators' drive to promote a European spirit, a strong shift towards the national and the local has occurred. The nature of directives (rather than regulations) that provide member states with expectations of implementing minimum standards does not assist this matter. However, attempts to transition minimum standards into full harmonization appear to be over-ambitious. The discussion about the Common European Sales Law (CESL)[2] that has spread over two decades is a case in point. The aim of uniform legislation of contract law throughout the legal traditions of the member states and to ensure the good functioning of the internal market has not found any agreement (Gomes 2015).

How can we build and maintain a system to help consumers facing similar problems in different legal settings? To build a system of ADR that is trusted by its users, and thus becomes a part of the national justice system, I believe we need to step back from the European ambitions and revisit the local/national context. Taking the example of ombudsman, ADR, and informal justice, I will argue that it is essential to revisit the national frame in order to create and grow a system of informal justice. The institutions of an informal justice system co-exist with the formal justice system and its representing authorities. As Chapters 2 and 3 demonstrated, this means very different things in different member states. Institutions of the informal justice system need to gain support and acceptance within the national context before we can begin to think about a transition and merging of meaning into the European space.

In light of this diversity, how can we best approach building an informal justice system? In Chapter 3, I suggested to understand the ombudsman in terms of a legal transplant that has developed within its national

[1]http://www.lisbon-treaty.org/wcm/the-lisbon-treaty.html.

[2]http://www.europarl.europa.eu/legislative-train/theme-connected-digital-single-market/file-common-european-sales-law.

context. Relocated into new settings the ombudsman model requires a flexible approach to the context in which it will resolve disputes. This shift and development of the model has happened alongside the changing relationship between the individual and the state. This proliferation of the ombudsman model (usually in the public sector) happened, in its own time, long before the European legislation on ADR (Creutzfeldt 2018). This means that member states have existing ombudsmen, and other ADR models, that have grown up within the existing legal system. We night argue that ADR providers have acquired a form of localization though adapting to their particular context (implying further questions about cause and effect in the relationship between the local context and the institution). This includes their jurisdiction, language, staff, procedures, the way in which the ombudsman is set up (Chapter 3), all this having grown and been targeted towards the specific national and local context. ADR legislation thus formalized a framework with which, at a minimum, ADR providers had to comply. Subsequently, ADR bodies mushroomed to satisfy EU requirements for national coverage. The result is that, on paper, most countries have implemented the legislation, but on the ground there remains confusion. One of the largest challenges is to build trust and legitimacy over time in a developing institution with no strong identity.

Legal socialization introduces and continuously reinforces values that people accept in terms of what is right, lawful, and legitimate. Our socialization influences and guides people towards what they want from various agents of a justice system and its authorities. What goes hand in hand with this are people's expectations of authorities and how to engage with them. As discussed in Chapter 4, fairness, trust, and legitimacy are essential in creating a system of institutions delivering ADR and thereby shaping the mechanisms that are collectively called an informal justice system. Borrowing from the experience of the formal justice system fairness helps secure long-term commitment in an institution while legitimacy is needed to help people recognize institutional authority. Legitimacy is a vital component of social institutions, practices and arrangements, not just for their long-term survival but also their day-to-day functioning (Jackson et al. 2012). Trust is related to both fairness and legitimacy in that it is built when an authority is experienced as fair and legitimate (Tyler and Huo 2002).

Each member state is faced with a different set of challenges when establishing its informal justice mechanisms. Three of these entwined challenges I will briefly mention here: legal, cultural, and political. Some countries faced lengthy procedures for changing existing laws to allow for the ADR directive to be implemented into national legislation (Spain and Italy, for example), while others (for instance, Germany, Italy and France) faced cultural challenges around introducing ADR into the national legal framework. The national pre-disposition to the importance of the role of the court, judges and the legal profession remains an obstacle to effectively embracing ADR. This is closely linked with the political mood. For most member states ADR/ODR is not a priority on the national political agenda.

In the UK, for example, the government set ADR as a matter of political importance in 2016 to empower consumers and citizens and make them feel protected when buying goods and services. A Green Paper was on its way that would have ensured an increase in government regulation of ADR providers. Then the UK voted to leave the EU and since then ADR has fallen by the wayside of the political agenda. In this context, I am using the term ADR in a broad sense to include the multitude of institutions that provide redress for consumers and citizens. However, the ADR I am addressing here inhabits a specific niche of consumer ADR that I have expanded so as to compare it with the ombudsman institutions that offer ADR in the public sector. Acknowledging their differences, I believe that insights can be gained by focusing on the research on expectations of consumer ADR and applying those to the public ADR context. Recall the discussion of this when responding to O'Brien's fears in Chapter 3.

With the aim of exposing challenges in the transition from national to European contexts, I will offer two examples: first, different organizational structures; and, second, EU-wide networks.

Domestic politics around ADR have produced different approaches to informal dispute resolution. This is institutionally visible through diverse organizational structures and the variety of available processes of existing ADR bodies. Inconsistent national approaches to ADR create a situation where ADR institutions need to mature, over time, into their national context. Presently, ADR bodies are vulnerable while they are on their developmental journey towards a recognizable system of informal justice, and at the mercy of national political priorities. Growing and defining ADR bodies in the national context leads to their social meaning being closely entwined with the national, rather than the European (Chapter 6). My data suggests that ombudsmen are established within their specific national context in line with the national culture's approach to dispute resolution. This is significantly different in Germany and the UK, for example. Whilst this context specificity is something to aim for in the development of an ADR identity in the national context, it will inevitably provide a further barrier to creating a European system, and so I believe that it would be preferable to encourage the development of a national ADR identity, before seeking to expand across many borders. Meanwhile, a shard understanding of what ADR is would slowly spread across borders.

While national informal justice systems are struggling to be created, recognized, and used, sector-specific EU-wide networks have been built in parallel. Two relevant examples are the financial ADR providers in FIN-NET and the energy ADR providers in NEON (Creutzfeldt 2016a). These pan-European specialized networks create a shared space for sector-specific exchange. Set up by the European Commission in 2001, FIN-NET[3] promotes cooperation among national ombudsman in financial services and offers consumers easy access to ADR procedures in cross-border disputes about the provision of financial services. NEON[4] aims to promote ADR in Europe, to encourage the protection and empowerment of energy consumers and to represent its members at European level. NEON also stresses the importance of exchange of information, experience and best practice.

Despite differences and limitations in their national jurisdiction, structure, set-up and variety of complaints, there is a shared consensus and principles that unite the ADR providers in these networks. They present an opportunity for learning from each other and to potentially share best practice, in a non-country-specific context. Returning to thinking about the transition from the national to the European, it might be best to promote ADR within its national context while focusing on the expansion of sector-specific networks, rather than aiming to create an EU-wide informal dispute resolution space. This initial national focus would provide an opportunity to develop a stronger national ADR identity while simultaneously promoting EU-wide sector-specific shared standards. The transition from national to European begs the question of whether there can be a 'European identity' for a justice system/dispute resolution mechanism (Risse 2010).

Delving briefly into the larger and related debate about a European identity per se, Martinotti and Steffanizzi (1998) found that many people who strongly identify with their nation-state also feel a sense of belonging to Europe (see also Duchesne and Frognier 1995). Can this finding be harnessed and applied to the ADR context? Theoretically, we strive to understand how new institutions affect or otherwise change people's social identities. How do institutions shape people's beliefs about who they are and to which communities they belong? Thus, the question arises here as to how people relate to their national identity and how that translates into other spaces, for example, the acceptance of ADR and its institutions/actors.

---

[3]https://ec.europa.eu/info/business-economy-euro/banking-and-finance/consumer-finance-and-payments/consumer-financial-services/financial-dispute-resolution-network-fin-net/fin-net-network/about-fin-net_en.

[4]http://www.neon-ombudsman.org.

Observations about identity could help understand how ADR institutions could grow at the national and local level to then expand into the European space. Herrmann et al. (2004) suggest three ways of thinking about multiple identities: as nested, as cross-cutting, and as separate. Nested identities can be thought of as one inside the other, with a core identity residing in the centre that permits outer circles of other identities—for example, a local identity at the core surrounded by a layer of national identity, nested in a layer of European identity. Cross-cutting identities are those relating to the idea of belonging to different groups. For example, a person can feel an ethnic identity and a sense of belonging to Europe, even though not all other members of that ethnic group will identify with Europe. Separate identities are those that have no overlap into group membership. Usually, the relationship between European and other identities is thought of to be cross-cutting or nested. They are not mutually exclusive. Within the nested model, a degree of hierarchy between people's sense of belonging and loyalties has been described at both the elite and mass public opinion levels. This puts the nation state at the core of our nested identities with 'European-ness' forming the outer layer. I argue that this is how we can approach ADR socialization, with a foundation in the national, then potentially entering a European space.

European institutions construct a post-national civic identity in the Habermasian sense (Habermas 1994, 1996), emphasizing democracy, human rights, market economy, the welfare state, and cultural diversity (Laffan 1996). Having said that, it is a challenge to attribute social meaning to and develop an identity with a European project that is constantly changing, developing, and without clear boundaries. For this reason, I consider it important to have a national framework, within which ADR can grow and be identifiable.

In sum, the national is a more digestible framework within which to understand ADR, especially when thinking about questions of justice. Is justice particularly tied to national cultures because it is intrinsically linked to normative assumptions about what is right or wrong or what is fair and unfair? This ties in closely with questions about what values and ethics are being promoted through an ombudsman/ADR process. Being 'fair and just' means to have rules that represent values, ethics and beliefs, including a transparent public process to enhance the use of and trust in ADR. Katch and Rabinovich-Einy (2017) argue that ADR delivers more access and less justice; more speed but less fairness.

Just ADR: Balancing Process and Outcome

Having focused on the institutional, national and European context of ADR, I now turn to the users of the system. What are their procedural needs and why does it matter? Let me start with answering the second part of that question first. It matters because of what users of the ADR system need and expect from its procedures, namely that it provides a user-friendly and accessible dispute resolution model. Directing the focus to the national context when thinking about the people who use ADR provides helpful insights. My empirical data expose the diversity of expectations of different ombudsman, even within a single national context. The range of expectations revealed by my data showed a generous amount of diversity accompanied by a lack of knowledge about the ombudsman process. How can we determine users' procedural needs? Further, how can we find the appropriate combination of process and outcome when designing dispute resolution procedures for a specific niche set of problem? I suggest a simple, twofold answer. First, we can assume that users (in different contexts and countries) of different types of ADR bodies want to be treated fairly, to be told what to expect from the process, and to get an outcome they think is fair. The distribution of importance of these elements differs. Second, procedural needs will vary according to: the type of complaint; the impact of the complaint on the day-to-day life of the complainant; the duration of the complaint; the age and education of the complainant; the financial and emotional value of the complaint, to name a few. It is impossible to grasp which of these factors are more influential, as they can change throughout a complaint journey and shift in prevalence in response to the stage of a complaint, in a similar fashion to the roles identified in Chapter 6. We are talking here about people as emotive beings, so a process that is responsive and flexible is important. This process needs to also fulfil criteria of fairness and provide outcomes that can be relied upon.

One example to illustrate the complexity and differences in expectations and perceptions of the mix of elements mentioned above is—generally speaking[5]—that of the perception of the duration of a complaint. A consumer who contacts the telecoms ombudsman to complain about her bills expects a speedy resolution and is likely to measure speed as an indicator for satisfaction that can then be transformed into trust. In contrast to this, a

[5]I offer here a generalization to highlight trends to understand procedural needs—of course there are procedural differences within the individual sectors and ombudsman procedures, as mentioned before.

citizen who approaches a public sector ombudsman with a complaint about a local hospital, for example, appears to be more willing to accept a longer wait for an outcome of her case. Even more, it seems that, whilst being updated about the complaint's progress, it is more likely that an outcome is deemed acceptable if she thinks sufficient time was spent on helping her with her claim. In that case, a speedy reply would have had the opposite effect. In these examples, it seems that satisfaction and trust would be produced in opposite ways. Does this mean that we use a different set of criteria to evaluate different forms of dispute resolution procedures (justice)? In an attempt to answer this question, I now return to the ideas of process justice and outcome justice.

Building on Chapter 5 in which I showed that procedural justice matters in the ombudsman context, I argue here that it only showcases one part of the bigger story accompanying people's complaint journeys. The vast literature on procedural justice helps us understand how the human need to be treated fairly during an interaction with an authority, then enables us to accept an unexpected outcome more easily. In the ombudsman context my data showed that, despite procedural justice being important to ombudsman users, the outcome still played a role in their overall perception of the process. What does this mean translated into ombudsman users' procedural needs? Does a process need to be built differently for different types of disputes? If we assume that procedures are geared towards justice (or the perception thereof) and outcomes towards settlement, what does that mean for different types of ADR providers?

In a dispute resolution scenario without constraints on financial considerations, timeliness, and different jurisdictions, conflicts would ideally be resolved by responding directly to their contextual complexity. To do this suitably, Menkel-Meadow (2004) reminds us that both cognitive and behavioural components are involved in conflict resolution. This lends itself to further thinking about the most appropriate path to resolve a dispute. If we understand the 'A' in ADR as appropriate, rather than alternative, it implies the search for a form of dispute resolution that offers a rich variety of settlement options—in and outside the formal court setting. Despite being suitable for certain types of disputes, the formal justice system is 'often inadequate for a fuller satisfaction of human needs and interests, and so we must look to other processes than traditional institutions or practices, depending on the kind of conflict or dispute at issue' (Menkel-Meadow 2004: 7). A pluralistic conception of justice with matching processes can be found in *process pluralism.* Here, Menkel-Meadow argues that despite procedural justice being significant for justice-seekers, it is also important to appreciate that some processes have an effect on the outcome. This resonates with the findings in Chapter 5, where my data showed that, despite procedural justice being important in the ombudsman context, the outcome cannot always clearly be seen as separate from the process. How then can we make the right process choices? Sander and Goldberg (1994) argue that *fitting the forum to the fuss* is about choosing the right or appropriate process to match the dispute. Fitting the forum to the fuss 'includes different kinds of fuss at different levels of society, including social, cultural and reparative' (Menkel-Meadow 2015: 4).

This US-based discourse is very much situated in the context of understanding ADR in the midst of a complex legal landscape as foremost as a form of dispute resolution that is adaptable to its context. Left with a multitude of choice of processes, individuals are typically assisted by lawyers, arbitrators, mediators or other experts to find the best 'fit' for them. We might see this as an opportunity for someone who can afford it to get help in choosing the procedure that would provide the best outcomes for a particular dispute. Whilst this approach shows that not all disputes should be dealt with in the same manner (Menkel-Meadow 2003), the accompanying bitter flavour of creating (yet another) system of justice for those who can afford it remains. Also, 'fitting the forum to the fuss' might be seen as a positive rendition of 'forum-shopping', which is usually presented as an obstacle to informal justice.

Nevertheless, the debate about finding the appropriate process for resolving a dispute can help with deliberations about how we think about ADR (and ombudsman) and their processes. The above, shamelessly brief summary of a long journey of ADR in the US literature demonstrates again that, when we talk about ADR, we can be describing very different things and, therefore, I propose that understanding ADR through context offers one way to have a productive conversation about process and outcomes. As a shared feature, what ADR (if appropriate or alternative) stands for in general terms is that it provides tools to resolve disputes outside of the formal court settings. These means, however, vary significantly as mentioned before. Hence, the ADR that the private sector ombudsman offer for consumers and the ADR that the public sector ombudsman offer for citizens come with different sets of procedural challenges, as well as synergies.

The similarity is that ADR providers in any sector offer an informal pathway for complaints that lie within their responsibility. I mention this, as it is very possible that some types of complaints are outside of the remit of ADR providers. A further similarity is that the processes usually involve little face-to-face human interaction and typically a complainant will not be assisted and guided through the process by a lawyer. Rather, the processes are intended for complainants to be able to manage to navigate themselves. Here might be the space to appreciate the limitations of ADR and to be realistic about what it can contribute and where its limitations lie. The anticipated outcome is a settlement about which both parties can come to an agreement. The ombudsman in both scenarios is providing a service to redress the imbalance of power between the individual and the state and between the individual and a company that the complaint has created between the parties.

Differences lie within the specific processes that the individual ADR providers offer. Generously grouped according to the type of complaints dealt with, these can be clustered into (whilst presenting procedural variations within): public and private sector ADR providers; sector-specific ADR providers (telecom, financial services, for example). Do all these differences provide for 'process pluralism' or just for confusion and potential dissatisfaction? I would argue that this multitude of different processes and outcomes does not represent process pluralism; rather it exposes an array of different existing procedural standards within a pre-determined set for a certain type of dispute. A citizen or consumer cannot choose the process they will be entering into, but rather they are signing up to the type of dispute resolution procedure the specific ADR provider offers. Consequently, how much of this process the user is part of depends on the type and complexity of their complaint as well as the ADR providers.

What, then, in this new dispute resolution environment is the appropriate combination of process and outcome when designing dispute resolution for a certain category of problems? The ADR model that is currently being promoted in the EU for small-value consumer complaints is suffering from a lack of identity. There are no shared values, norms, or identifiable structures. One inherent and reoccurring difficulty that most member states face in encouraging the informal justice system to flourish is that of funding. The ADR providers I have focused on in this volume are typically free of charge for consumers (and for citizens using public sector ombudsman). This creates two related challenges. First, a challenge for ADR providers with a variety of funding structures. For some ADR providers it is a challenge to offer consistent, high quality procedural standards and outcomes when faced with growing consumer demands for procedural justice, timeliness, and fair outcomes. Many ADR providers lack sufficient numbers of staff with appropriate training. While most ADR providers have developed in-house training for their staff, it would be beneficial, in support of developing an ADR identity, to offer (accredited) training for all who work for ADR bodies, to promote shared standards and shared procedural quality. The next step would therefore be to develop a clear training and professional career path for individuals employed in ADR bodies.

The challenge concerns the effect on users of the ADR system. If an individual approaches an ADR body and does not receive the expected level of attention, this will inevitably harm the already fragile relationship between the user and the ADR provider. As mentioned before, the initial contact a user has with the ADR system usually sets the tone for the remainder of the interaction. This means that if the user is not met with enough care, attention and expectations management at the outset, the procedural experience will have got off to a bad start. In some cases this supports users' suspicions that ADR providers are actually working for the companies about what they have complained. Similarly, users who have had an unsatisfying experience during interaction with public sector ombudsman can equate this feeling with being let down by public administration and the state (Creutzfeldt and Bradford 2016).

Generally speaking, my data on ombudsmen in Germany and the UK have provided empirical evidence for users of ADR providers valuing procedural fairness. Despite difficulties in clearly discerning process experience from outcome experience (as has been shown in various other quantitatively studied contexts), there are lessons that can be learned. Within the boundaries of the ADR context discussed in this book I propose to consider process and outcome from the following premises.

First, *procedural justice matters to users of the ADR system.* ADR providers could train staff who interact with individuals early on in the complaints process and enable them to deal with the emotive, behavioural and factual elements of a dispute. This would produce greater appreciation of the ADR process and increase user satisfaction. Although this would be an added financial investment on the part of the ADR provider, it would deliver the long-term goals of building trust and user satisfaction, and having fewer complaints escalate through the system. This would reduce the overall cost for the ADR provider as well as helping to restore customer loyalty towards the business.

Second, *outcomes do matter.* If a process is perceived to be fair, then outcomes are more readily accepted, even if they are not those that were expected when originally bringing the complaint to an ADR provider. Although, as I explored in Chapter 5, outcomes do play a role in the ADR context, it does not hurt to acknowledge (a common-sense fact) that, if we feel that we are being treated fairly, we will more readily accept an outcome. So, if outcomes are geared towards settlement, then a perceived fair process is more likely to support this.

In sum, it seems beneficial for individual ADR providers to deliver reliable procedures and outcomes in striving towards the overall ambition of establishing a trusted model of ADR. Whilst plausible in theory, the everyday practice of ADR has shown this to be a real challenge. Confronted with a plethora of approaches and widespread user confusion, I believe we have to engage in a discussion about appropriate process design. As Genn has said:

> In order to design appropriate court alternatives outside of the commercial field, consideration must be given to: the nature of the dispute or grievance at issue and the range of possible outcomes; the balance of resources between the parties in terms of finance, experience and competence; and the complexity of the relevant law. Consideration must also be given to the training of those who preside over informal proceedings (Genn 1993: 411).

We need to ask the same questions of ADR providers, as of other providers of dispute resolution, about who accesses them, who evaluates them, and who is accountable for them. Every system creates its own problems and the current landscape of ADR with its functional and regulatory gaps creates space for misuse. For example, at present the ADR landscape allows for repeat players, forum-shopping, and businesses making dubious use of people's data.[6] Perhaps it would be worthwhile to look at the various ADR providers' systems design to better understand existing flaws and to find solutions for them. Part of this involves closely looking at whether the system currently being developed actually meets its users' needs. It appears to me that most ADR procedures are still the preserve of those who have the ability to navigate the system.

Beyond a System for People 'Like Us'

The structure of ADR that is developing in the EU to help consumers access processes to solve their complaints is not promoting access to justice as a public good. Rather, with this model, access to justice appears to be reserved for the few. ADR is not as visible, and therefore not accessed as much, as was initially anticipated. It produces a complex set of procedural and outcome

[6]Making use of the complex ADR landscape, some companies have made it their business to assist consumers in finding the way through the maze and directing them to an ADR provider. To do this in the most beneficial manner, the individual has to provide personal data, which then is used to contact the company as well as being stored for detecting trends and consumer behavior.

expectations that potential users are not accustomed to. For those who do access ADR, the process can be challenging in that expectations are not managed well and people do not always feel fairly treated. Remember that a person who reaches out to an ADR body has already been through an unsuccessful complaints process with the company or service provider and is therefore typically in an emotionally charged state. To navigate ADR procedures takes a certain amount of determination and stamina and the system that has evolved tends to suit the most *able* individuals and remains inaccessible to vulnerable individuals and other less-able groups—the invisibles.

What is to be done for these invisibles who cannot use or access the system? Because these groups are not currently accessing ADR, it is difficult to grasp why this is the case. More research needs to be done to explore why access to justice in this context seems to mean access for the selected few and not the masses. Does this mean that ADR is a 'second class' or inferior form of justice, which has found popularity in the EU and at national level to save money? I do not believe that to be the case. Rather I argue that ADR is in desperate need of an identity, developed within its particular national context with shared standards, values and ethics. The differing structures, funding models, remit, and accountability of ADR bodies poses a huge challenge to the anticipated aim of finding a shared identity in order to gain legitimacy and build trust.

A real challenge for the expanding ADR model is for it to be accessible to the ordinary individual and disadvantaged or vulnerable person. Procedures need to be flexible enough to cater for different types of users. This will have direct implications, for example, funding and staff training in each ADR provider. Adapting to users' needs and capabilities and providing just and fair procedures and outcomes takes focused investment. In many ways it seems that ADR, encouraging a cheap, fast, accessible and easy path to redress, might just not be the right path for everyone—or for every type of dispute.

I would now like to return to the discussion begun earlier in this volume (Chapter 3) about legal culture and the significance of the national context to a developing ADR model. If we think about creating ADR procedures that are tailored not only to the masses but that also cater for the individual, legal culture offers a good starting point. By understanding legal culture as emerging from an interactive process between meaning and the social and cultural practices of everyday life (Marshall 2006: 237), we can transfer this onto to thinking about how best to tailor an ADR process to meet people's expectations and needs. Returning to how ordinary people make sense of (legal) procedures in their everyday lives, legal consciousness forms a part of our cultural toolkit. By taking our existing frames of legality, set around our own experiences, we are able to create new meanings for them and thereby expand them. This is how ADR could be slowly incorporated into the catalogue of meanings that we use to make sense of our encounters with authorities in the legal system. In addition, if this is done in a consistent manner, ADR providers would gain legitimacy, earn trust and be accepted and recognized as institutions in their own right in the developing informal justice system.

Conclusions

In this chapter, I have invited readers to think about informal justice from different angles. Starting from the European legislators' initiative to shape an informal justice system that allows European citizens to discover ADR, I have suggested considering informal dispute resolution more generally. I have also proposed that the debate be situated in the national context rather than the European one.

As there is currently no shared ADR identity, language, procedure, understanding or acceptance, I suggest that thinking about ADR in the national context is the more productive option. For ADR to work and for it to be accepted it needs to develop from the inside-out. Because each national context is different and has developed, within its own legal culture, a socialization and an expectation of its legal authorities, I believe that it is premature to think about a shared ADR identity or to even start to generalize what type of justice or fairness ADR is providing. There are multiple factors constraining the national implementation of ADR bodies, for example, politics surrounding the introduction of ADR, the acceptance of different approaches to ADR, and finding the best way to regulate the market for ADR providers.

The ADR system that is evolving needs to fit its varied users' needs. Procedures and outcomes need to be accessible, transparent, fair, reasonably speedy and somewhat consistent. The development of an informal justice system is well underway, but it is being stunted in its popular expansion by the realities of its national contexts. For this reason, I suggest harnessing the differences to adapt ADR bodies to their national setting and thereby to create an ADR identity, or even culture. Only then would it be possible to discover what this might mean for the development of an informal justice system across Europe.

9

Conclusion: Paths for Theory and Research

Experiencing Informal Justice Through a Cultural Lens

In this book, I explored how ordinary people experience informal justice. I provided fresh insights into dispute resolution in a cross-national context. I focussed my inquiry on people's expectations of one of the most developed models providing ADR: the ombudsman.

I collected an original set of empirical data from ombudsman users in Germany and the UK. The database allowed me to test and compare theories, tease out narratives, and thereby to explore the development of informal justice in Europe. Appreciating the complexity of human decision-making, I chose to move beyond a purely quantitative or purely qualitative approach to understand how our behaviour is motivated. To achieve this I combined the rapidly developing literature on procedural justice and legal consciousness. This approach allowed me to gain a more holistic understanding of people's expectations and interactions with ADR. Thinking about how our legal socialization contributes to our understanding of how we make sense of the ADR process, construct ideas about justice, and make decisions about legitimacy provided a fruitful background. I develop the argument throughout the chapters of this book that our consciousness around 'alternatives' to formal legality is rooted in our national legal socialization and lived (and constantly redefined) through our legal consciousness. Why does this matter? Because it helps us to understand better where the notions of fairness and justice that we draw upon when faced with an

N. Creutzfeldt, *Ombudsmen and ADR*, Palgrave Socio-Legal Studies,
https://doi.org/10.1007/978-3-319-78807-4_9

institution that we are not familiar with originate. It can also help understand how we generate trust in a developing institution. I argue that the relationships people have with the informal justice system are shaped by their experiences and preconceptions about how the (formal) legal system and its agents behave and fulfil that role.

This brings the focus to the national context. The way in which we accept ADR (or not) is guided by our nationally developed relationships with authority and our formal justice system. In other words, I suggest that our expectations are not formed by the ADR providers—due to lack of exposure and socialization—but, rather, they are guided by our pre-existing attitudes towards the formal system. To measure the uptake, impact, and acceptance of ombudsman we use concepts that are familiar and accepted, such as justice, fairness, legitimacy and trust. Different types of ombudsman serve different sectors and have different functions, but essentially they are all part of a large ADR landscape. In order to assess if such a thing as ADR socialization (identity) exists, or if it is a worthwhile endeavour to strive towards, we need to look at the national context where we find distinct patterns of ADR in each member state. Although there are sector-specific ombudsman that might deal with the same type of complaints in different countries, they are likely to have different procedures to reach the respective outcomes. As I have demonstrated through my data, a popular understanding of justice informs people's expectations of ombudsman and ADR. This, in turn, creates social meanings of ombudsman and ADR situated in a national context. ADR is usually added to an existing justice system to fill gaps, to allow for access to justice, yet does not seem to be able to move out of the shadow of the formal system to be seen as a force in its own right. For it to come out of the shadow it needs to develop its own identity. This is in itself a challenge.

I argue that we need to grow and focus on ADR within the national context and only then it might mature into a European space. Individual chapters offered some critical implications for thinking about informal justice, ADR, and ombudsman in particular. Here I would like to offer some reflections or the future development of researching informal justice in Europe. I focus on three related areas: ombudsman and ADR design, vulnerable users, and the challenges of the digital.

Ombudsman/ADR Design

ADR, at its best, contributes to access to justice and has the potential to be a model of dispute resolution that embraces our values of what a just and fair procedure looks like. ADR models then ideally have to be designed to reflect values and ethical standards that go hand in hand with our attitudes. The main issue to be approached is the uneven set of procedures that ADR providers offer in each member state. The lack of consistent national regulations hinders a harmonised development of ADR. How to best bridge this gap in the existing imbalanced regulatory structure? Setting out to write a book about European justice systems, following excitedly the anticipated spread of informal justice throughout the member states as a result of the EU wide regulations on ADR and ODR, I have continually had to return to exploring and understanding the national context. I gather that this is the result of trying to study what a large concept as informal justice means in a European context. Deconstructing Europe into its individual member states seemed the most productive approach to understand the development of informal justice.

I return to the national context and, this time, even closer to the actual procedures, by looking at the ombudsman/ADR providers themselves. What I have not focused on in great detail in this book is the question of dispute systems design (Gill et al. 2016; Le Sueur 2012; Amsler et al. 2015). Exploring how forms, functions, and limits of dispute processes combine to deliver effective justice (Fuller 2001) is a valuable exercise to move a system that provides dispute resolution closer to its users' needs. Ideally, a dispute resolution system is designed to not only provide effective and efficient processes from an institutional perspective, but also for the users of the process. Further inquiry is needed into understanding how to maximise the processes to provide appropriate systems for the disputes with which ombudsmen deal with. This leads to the next point, we have to not only think about who uses the system but also more focus on who does not use the system and why.

Vulnerable Groups

As I have outlined in previous chapters, ADR bodies—designed to enable access to justice *for all*—is in reality rather restricted *to a few*. This means that an ordinary individual or disadvantaged (vulnerable) person will not find ADR to be easily accessible or user-friendly. Procedures need to be flexible enough to cater for different types of users. Again, our empirical knowledge about the value of ADR approaches, particularly in relation to access to justice and vulnerability, remains very thin. The data I collected shows a pattern of ombudsman users, that is also reflected in ombudsman annual reports: they are typically male (white), educated, and in their mid 50s. More work needs to be done to understand why only certain groups of the population find their way to the ombudsman and what to do about it.

It seems to me that the current set up of ADR providers does not appropriately cater for a diverse range of users. Whilst this is also a process design question, the most obvious reason for that seems to be budgetary restrictions along with meeting expectations of speedy dispute resolution. I fear that the way in which ADR bodies are aiming to meet their performance indicators, are adapting online as a platform to communicate through rather than phone interactions, and are pressured by time limits, does not suit a complainant who is not able to navigate and online format or understand how to engage with the process. A few ombudsmen have developed special units that are dedicated to look after complainants that require special attention and time. This requires an interaction with and reaching out to agencies that are also in touch with these vulnerable individuals to provide the best support. This is a measure that most ombudsmen will not be able to afford. What does this mean for access to justice for all—at the moment ombudsmen are not able to provide this convincingly. We need to be able to better understand the intricacies and challenges of how best to serve vulnerable groups and thus provide access to ADR—but which form might this take? In a new project we will explore these questions looking at the European energy sector.[1]

Besides thinking about the most appropriate process design and how vulnerable groups can be supported and helped to access justice through ombudsmen/ADR, we also need to think about how our surroundings have evolved.

[1] https://esrcjustenergy.wordpress.com.

Challenge of the Digital—Future Research into the New Everyday

Living in the age of sharing economy, the internet, a trip adviser mentality of rankings, expecting instant responses, artificial intelligence and algorithms, we need to rethink our approach to making sense of and studying these new spaces. The shift to algorithms and big data determining our everyday has already happened as a subtle by-product of managing our lives online (subscriptions and online shopping, for example). Algorithms and big data challenge the notion of process fairness, outcome fairness and procedural quality control.

These developments bring with them challenges to existing ADR models as well as the need to create new ones that are fit for the digital space. The possibilities seem endless when entertaining the thought of regulating online spaces, making the internet safe for us to use and navigate without being stripped of our identity. Thinking about justice, fairness, trust and legitimacy thus begs us first to critically evaluate our roles and values within our justice system to then challenge them in the new context. Might they have to be reconsidered? Do we need new measures and tools to create appropriate protection for actors and users in these new and rapidly growing spaces? How can we best understand these areas of little regulation and complexity that cannot fully be captured by traditional methods, models, and language?

I suggest to explore the theoretical and empirical dimension of these complex new spaces we need both interdisciplinary approaches and methodological pluralism. We need to be creative in our approach to understanding how people and law intersect and explore new spaces that are created. Understanding law in everyday life becomes more than an inquiry into what people experience as law and how they translate this experience into actions. It becomes a nuanced and layered inquiry into how and through which channels people make sense of different processes. Only then will we be able to detect emerging and new patterns of legal consciousness, a form of ADR socialization, a *European turn* of dispute resolution and procedural justice.

I think we need to generate space for new models of dispute resolution to create their own terminology and lens through which we will be able to understand developments in these potentially fluid dispute resolution spaces. This calls for a confident stride towards combining methods and disciplines to grasp the legal, the social, the cultural, and *the new.*

Annex

Your experience with Ombudsman Services: Energy

Thank you for agreeing to participate in this survey. The aim of this short anonymous survey is to get a better understanding of how you experienced dealing with Ombudsman Services: Energy (OS: Energy). What did you value and what could be improved? The survey will help develop the experience of dealing with an ombudsman service and inform future change.

The order of questions aims to reflect your complaint journey: before you contacted the ombudsman/ first contact / the procedure / the outcome / and overall experience.

All survey responses are confidential, and will be used for research purposes only.

You can also choose to complete this survey online at:
https://www.survey.bris.ac.uk/oxford/ose

This survey will not take longer than 10 minutes to complete.

Before you contacted Ombudsman Services

1. **When did the problem, you contacted Ombudsman Services about first start?**
   [Month/year] ______________________

2. **Could you briefly state, in your own words, what the problem was you contacted Ombudsman Services about?**

3. **I feel that I have spent much time and effort on trying to sort out the problem before approaching the ombudsman.**

   [ ] Strongly agree   [ ] Agree   [ ] Neither agree or disagree   [ ] disagree   [ ] strongly disagree

   …and what did you expect Ombudsman Services to do for you?

N. Creutzfeldt, *Ombudsmen and ADR*, Palgrave Socio-Legal Studies,
https://doi.org/10.1007/978-3-319-78807-4

4. How important were the following in your decision to complain?

	1 most important – 5 least important				
	1	2	3	4	5
Resolving my problem	[ ]	[ ]	[ ]	[ ]	[ ]
Getting someone to listen to me	[ ]	[ ]	[ ]	[ ]	[ ]
Getting an apology	[ ]	[ ]	[ ]	[ ]	[ ]
Getting a financial award and / or my money back	[ ]	[ ]	[ ]	[ ]	[ ]
Changing the business processes	[ ]	[ ]	[ ]	[ ]	[ ]
Preventing others from having the same problems as myself	[ ]	[ ]	[ ]	[ ]	[ ]
Being treated with respect and dignity	[ ]	[ ]	[ ]	[ ]	[ ]
To get an impartial view on my problem	[ ]	[ ]	[ ]	[ ]	[ ]
To get what is lawfully mine, without having to pay.	[ ]	[ ]	[ ]	[ ]	[ ]

First contact with Ombudsman Services: Energy

5. Is this the first time that you are dealing with an ombudsman service?
[ ] yes [ ] no

6. How did you hear about Ombudsman Services?

[ ] From the company complained about
[ ] Deadlock letter from company
[ ] 8 week letter from company
[ ] Ombudsman Services website
[ ] Internet search
[ ] Media (newspaper, radio, TV)
[ ] Recommended (friend, family, colleague)
[ ] other, please specify

7. How did you first contact OS: Energy?

[ ] by telephone
[ ] by letter / fax
[ ] by email
[ ] Through Ombudsman Services website
[ ] Someone else contacted on my behalf
[ ] Social media (Facebook / twitter)
[ ] other, please specify

8. When did you first contact OS: Energy?
[Month/year] ______________________________

9. **What was your impression of the STAFF when you first contacted OS: Energy?** *Choose as many as apply…*

[ ] helpful
[ ] understood my problem
[ ] seemed to know what they were talking about
[ ] treated me with respect and courtesy
[ ] seemed trustworthy / seemed to act with good intent
[ ] seemed interested in hearing my story
[ ] seemed unbiased and neutral
[ ] were unhelpful
[ ] did not understand my problem
[ ] not sure, can't remember

10. Did you ever use the ombudsman's website?

[ ] yes [ ] no

… if you did, how easy or difficult was it to find what you needed on OS: Energy's website?

[ ] very easy **[ ] fairly easy** **[ ] neither easy nor difficult** **[ ] fairly difficult** **[ ] very difficult**

The procedure

The following questions are aimed at understanding how you experienced the stages in the decision-making procedure and how you felt about the way your case was handled, **before you received an outcome.**

11. Were you satisfied with how OS: Energy dealt with your case?

[ ] Very satisfied [ ] Fairly satisfied [ ] Neither satisfied nor dissatisfied [ ] Fairly dissatisfied [ ] Very dissatisfied

12. Was the way in which your case was decided what you expected?

[ ] Exactly what I expected [ ] Close to what I expected [ ] Not sure what I expected [ ] Not at all what I expected

13. During the procedure dealing with OS: Energy (before you got the outcome) would you agree or disagree that …

	Strongly agree	Agree	Neither agree or disagree	Disagree	Strongly disagree
The information you received was accurate	[ ]	[ ]	[ ]	[ ]	[ ]
You were kept informed about how your case was progressing	[ ]	[ ]	[ ]	[ ]	[ ]
You felt the time it took to reach a decision was appropriate	[ ]	[ ]	[ ]	[ ]	[ ]
You felt that you had your say in the procedure	[ ]	[ ]	[ ]	[ ]	[ ]
You felt that your case handler understood your problem	[ ]	[ ]	[ ]	[ ]	[ ]
You felt that your case handler took you seriously	[ ]	[ ]	[ ]	[ ]	[ ]
You felt the case handler was neutral	[ ]	[ ]	[ ]	[ ]	[ ]
You were treated with respect and courtesy	[ ]	[ ]	[ ]	[ ]	[ ]
You felt you could trust the case handler	[ ]	[ ]	[ ]	[ ]	[ ]
The communication from the case handler was easy to understand	[ ]	[ ]	[ ]	[ ]	[ ]

14. How did you mostly communicate with Ombudsman Services?

[ ] telephone conversation
[ ] correspondence by post
[ ] through someone else
[ ] portal
[ ] emailing
[ ] internet (excluding email)

15. Were you happy with the method of communication?

[ ] Very happy [ ] Fairly happy [ ] Neither happy nor unhappy [ ] Fairly unhappy [ ] Very unhappy

16. How many times do you estimate were you in contact (email, telephone, letter, fax…) with the ombudsman team throughout the complaints procedure?

[ ] Up to 10 times [ ] Between 10–20 times [ ] More than 20 times [ ] I am not sure

17. How long did you expect the procedure to take?

[ ] Less than one month [ ] 1–3 months [ ] More than 3 months

18. How long did it actually take?

[ ] Less than one month [ ] 1–3 months [ ] More than 3 months

The outcome

The following questions are about the outcome of your case, and how you experienced it.

19. Do you know at what stage in the OS: Energy procedure your case finished?

[ ] Early resolution - facilitated by ombudsman team
[ ] Settlement- agreed over the phone
[ ] Ombudsman decision -agreed in writing
[ ] Not sure
[ ] OTHER, please specify:

20. Was the outcome of your case In your favour?

[ ] yes [ ] no [ ] partially [ ] no sure

21. Was the outcome what you expected?

[ ] Exactly what I expected [ ] Close to what I expected [ ] Not sure what I expected [ ] Not at all what I expected

22. Were you willing to accept the outcome?

[ ] Very willing [ ] Fairly willing [ ] Neither willing nor unwilling [ ] Fairly unwilling [ ] Very unwilling

23. If you are unwilling to accept the outcome, what will you do next? I plan to take my case …

[ ] … to a court
[ ] … involve a lawyer
[ ] … write a letter to MP
[ ] … I will take no further action
[ ] … involve another body (please specify)
[ ] … other, please specify

24. Considering the outcome of your case would you agree or disagree that

	Strongly agree	Agree	Neither agree or disagree	Disagree	Strongly disagree
The outcome of my case was explained clearly	[ ]	[ ]	[ ]	[ ]	[ ]
The outcome was fair and unbiased	[ ]	[ ]	[ ]	[ ]	[ ]
I understand why OS: Energy reached this decision.	[ ]	[ ]	[ ]	[ ]	[ ]
The procedure was transparent	[ ]	[ ]	[ ]	[ ]	[ ]
The length of time it took to deal with my case felt appropriate	[ ]	[ ]	[ ]	[ ]	[ ]

25. Do you think that others with a similar complaint as yours receive the same outcome from OS: Energy?

[ ] Yes [ ] Likely [ ] Not sure [ ] Probably not [ ] No

26. Do you feel that you had any control over the outcome?

[ ] Yes [ ] Likely [ ] Not sure [ ] Probably not [ ] No

27. Which of the following statements applies to you?

	Yes	Very likely	Not sure	Probably not	No
I feel a moral obligation to follow OS: Energy's recommendation	[ ]	[ ]	[ ]	[ ]	[ ]
I have confidence in OS: Energy	[ ]	[ ]	[ ]	[ ]	[ ]
The OS: Energy acting according to the law	[ ]	[ ]	[ ]	[ ]	[ ]

The overall experience with OS:Energy

For the following questions please think about your overall experience with dealing with the ombudsman service, from first contact to outcome of your case.

28. Throughout the experience of dealing with the ombudsman service would you say that the *people* who dealt with your complaint:

	Strongly agree	Agree	Neither agree or disagree	Disagree	Strongly disagree
Always did what they said they would	[ ]	[ ]	[ ]	[ ]	[ ]
Understood your problem	[ ]	[ ]	[ ]	[ ]	[ ]
You felt confident that they had the authority to deal with your problem	[ ]	[ ]	[ ]	[ ]	[ ]
It was easy to get in touch with the person handling your case	[ ]	[ ]	[ ]	[ ]	[ ]
The people dealing with my case knew what they were talking about	[ ]	[ ]	[ ]	[ ]	[ ]
The people dealing with my case seemed to be impartial	[ ]	[ ]	[ ]	[ ]	[ ]
The people dealing with my case seemed to have the same sense of right and wrong as I do	[ ]	[ ]	[ ]	[ ]	[ ]

29. How fair are the procedures the OS: Energy used to make the decision about your case?

[ ] Very fair [ ] Somewhat fair [ ] Not sure [ ] Somewhat unfair [ ] Very unfair

30. How likely are you to recommend OS: Energy to someone in a similar position to yourself?

[ ] Very likely [ ] Likely [ ] Not sure [ ] Unlikely [ ] Very unlikely

31. Overall, how satisfied were you with OS: Energy in general?

[ ] Very satisfied [ ] Somewhat satisfied [ ] Not sure [ ] Somewhat dissatisfied [ ] Very dissatisfied

32. Would you be comfortable sharing your case details for the purposes of improving the service offered by OS, if asked to complete a similar survey in the future?

[ ] yes [ ] no

Do you have any other comments about the way in which Ombudsman Services dealt with your case (i.e. what was good or what could be improved)?

Finally, about yourself

The following questions about you will help to identify if the ombudsman service is successful at reaching people from all backgrounds and treats everyone fairly and equally.

Are you: [ ] male [ ] female

Are you

[ ] Employed
[ ] Self-employed
[ ] Studying
[ ] Retired
[ ] Unable to work
[ ] Out of work and looking for work
[ ] Out of work but not currently looking for work
[ ] A homemaker
[ ] Other

What is the highest level of education you have completed?

[ ] 1-4 GCSEs (or equivalent)
[ ] Five or more GCSEs (or equivalent)
[ ] Two or more A-levels (or equivalent)
[ ] Skills for Life (including Basic Skills, Key Skills, Entry Level Certificates).
[ ] Diploma or equivalent
[ ] Bachelor degree or equivalent
[ ] Master degree or equivalent
[ ] Doctoral degree
[ ] Other

How old are you? [_________]

Do you have any long-standing illness, disability or infirmity? By long-standing we mean anything that has troubled you over a period of time or that is likely to affect you over a period of time?

[ ] yes, limited a lot [ ] yes, limited a little [ ] no

To which of these ethnic groups do you consider you belong?

[ ] white British
[ ] Any other white background
[ ] Mixed White and Black Caribbean
[ ] Mixed White and Black African
[ ] Mixed White and Asian
[ ] Any other mixed background
[ ] Indian
[ ] Pakistani
[ ] Bangladeshi
[ ] Any other Asian background
[ ] Black Caribbean
[ ] any other black background
[ ] Chinese
[ ] other ethnic group
[ ] prefer not to say

Thank you very much for taking the time to complete this survey.

Bibliography

Abraham, A. 2008. The Ombudsman and 'Paths to Justice': A Just Alternative or Just an Alternative? *Public Law* (1): 1–10.

Adler, Michael. 2006. Fairness in Context. *Journal of Law and Society* 33 (3): 615.

Adler, Michael. 2013. The Rise and Fall of Administrative Justice: A Cautionary Tale. *Socio Legal Review* 8 (2): 28–54.

Administrative Justice Steering Group. 2009. *The Way Forward—The Final Report of the Administrative Justice Steering Group*. Glasgow: Consumer Focus Scotland.

Aleinikoff, T. Alexander, and Douglas Klusmeyer (eds.). 2001. *Citizenship Today: Global Perspectives and Practices*. Washington, DC: Carnegie Endowment for International Peace.

Alexander, N.M. et al. 2005. *Mediation, Schlichtung, Verhandlungsmanagement: Formen der Konsensualer Streitbeilegung*, 1st ed. Münster: Alpman Schmidt.

Alexy, Robert. 1990. Grundrechte als subjektive Rechte und als objektive Normen. *Der Staat* 29 (1): 49–68.

Alleweldt, F. et al. (Civic Consulting). 2011. Cross-Border Alternative Dispute Resolution in the European Union. Brussels: European Parliament. http://www.europarl.europa.eu/meetdocs/2009_2014/documents/imco/dv/adr_study_/adr_study_en.pdf.

Almond, Gabriel Abraham, and Sidney Verba. 2015. *The Civic Culture: Political Attitudes and Democracy in Five Nations*. Princeton: Princeton University Press.

Amin, Ash, and Nigel Thrift. 1995. Globalization, Institutions, and Regional Development in Europe. EconPapers. Oxford University Press Catalogue, Oxford University Press. Accessed 14 November 2017.

Barrett-Howard, E., and T.R. Tyler. 1986. Procedural Justice as a Criterion in Allocation Decisions. *Journal of Personality and Social Psychology* 50: 296–304.

N. Creutzfeldt, *Ombudsmen and ADR*, Palgrave Socio-Legal Studies,
https://doi.org/10.1007/978-3-319-78807-4

Beek, Elke. 2007. The Slow Implementation of EC Directives. BS thesis, University of Twente. Accessed 14 November 2017. http://essay.utwente.nl/767/.

Beetham, David. 1991. *The Legitimation of Power*. Basingstoke: Palgrave Macmillan.

Behrens, Rob. 2012. Public Trust and the Ombudsman: The Case of the OIA. *Journal of Public Law and Policy* 83 (2): 1.

Behrens, Rob. 2015a. *Public Trust and the Ombudsman: The Case of the OIA*. Reading: Office of the Independent Adjudicator.

Behrens, Rob. 2015b. *Public Trust and the Ombudsman: The Case of the OIA*. The Office of the Independent Adjudicator. http://www.oiahe.org.uk/media/98008/public-trust-and-the-ombudsman-10th-anniversary-series.pdf.

Belin, Christof. 2014. *Alternative Streitbeilegung in Verbraucherkonflikten: Qualitätskriterien, Interssen, Best Practise*. Baden-Baden: Nomos.

Bercovitch, J., and A. Houston. 1985. Toward Another View of Legal Negotiation: The Structure of Problem-Solving. *UCLA Law Review* 31: 754–842.

Beyer, Peter. 1994. *Religion and Globalization*. London: Sage.

Bindman, Dan. 2017. Plan for 28-Month Online Court Pilot Emerges as MR Foresees Live-streaming Court of Appeal. Legal Futures. Accessed 14 November 2017. http://www.legalfutures.co.uk/latest-news/plan-28-month-online-court-pilot-emerges-mr-foresees-live-streaming-court-appeal.

Bingham, Tom. 2011. *The Rule of Law by Tom Bingham*. London: Penguin.

Blader, Steven L., and Tom R. Tyler. 2003. A Four-Component Model of Procedural Justice: Defining the Meaning of a "Fair" Process. *Personality and Social Psychology Bulletin* 29 (6): 747–758.

Blankenburg, Erhard. 1997. *Patterns of Legal Culture: The Netherlands Compared to Neighbouring Germany*. Amsterdam: Duitsland Instituut and Universiteit van Amsterdam.

Bottoms, Anthony, and Justice Tankebe. 2012. Criminology: Beyond Procedural Justice: A Dialogic Approach to Legitimacy in Criminal Justice. *Journal of Criminological Law and Criminology* 102: 119–170.

Bradford, Ben. 2014. Policing and Social Identity: Procedural Justice, Inclusion and Cooperation Between Police and Public. *Policing and Society* 24 (1): 22–43.

Bradford, Ben, and Jonathan Jackson. 2010. Different Things to Different People? The Meaning and Measurement of Trust and Confidence in Policing Across Diverse Social Groups in London. SSRN Scholarly Paper ID 1628546. Social Science Research Network, Rochester, NY. http://papers.ssrn.com/abstract=1628546.

Bradford, Ben, Jonathan Jackson, and Mike Hough. 2013. Police Legitimacy in Action: Lessons for Theory and Practice. SSRN Scholarly Paper ID 2236691. Social Science Research Network, Rochester, NY. http://papers.ssrn.com/abstract=2236691.

Bradford, B., and N. Creutzfeldt. 2018. Procedural Justice in Cross-Cultural Context: Fairness Judgements Among Users of Financial Ombuds Services in Germany and the United Kingdom (*Journal for Law in Society*—under review).

Braithwaite, Valerie. 2014. Defiance and Motivational Postures. In *Encyclopedia of Criminology and Criminal Justice*, ed. D. Weisburd and G. Bruinsma, 915–925. New York: Springer Verlag.

Buck, T., R. Kirkham, and B. Thompson. 2011. *The Ombudsman Enterprise and Administrative Justice*. Burlington, VT: Ashgate.

Cantwell, Brian, and Marian Roberts. 2016. *Marian Roberts,* Mediation in Family Disputes: Principles of Practice (4th ed.). *Journal of Social Work* 16 (2): 258–259.

Cappelletti, Mauro (ed.). 1981. *Access to Justice and the Welfare State*. Alphen aan den Rijn: European University Institute/Sijthoff/Giuffre.

Cappelletti, Mauro. 1993. Alternative Dispute Resolution Processes Within the Framework of the World-Wide Access-to-Justice Movement. *Modern Law Review* 56 (3): 282–296.

Cappelletti, Mauro, and Bryant Garth. 1977. Access to Justice: The Newest Wave in the Worldwide Movement to Make Rights Effective. *Buffalo Law Review* 27: 181.

Cappelletti, Mauro, and Bryant Garth (eds.). 1978. *Access to Justice: A World Survey*. Vol. 1 of the Florence Access to Justice Project Series. Alphen vaan den Rijn: Sijthoff/Giuffre.

Casper, J.D., T.R. Tyler, and B. Fisher. 1988. Procedural Justice in Felony Cases. *Law and Society Review* 22: 483–507.

Civil Justice Council. (2015). *Online Dispute Resolution for Low Value Civil Claims*. Online Dispute Resolution Advisory Group. Accessed 14 November 2017. https://www.judiciary.gov.uk/wp-content/uploads/2015/02/Online-Dispute-Resolution-Final-Web-Version1.pdf.

Clothier, C. 1986. The Value of an Ombudsman. *Public Law*, (summer edition): 204–211.

Cohn, Ellen S., and Susan O. White. 2012. *Legal Socialization: A Study of Norms and Rules*. New York: Springer Science & Business Media.

Coicaud, Jean-Marc. 2002. *Legitimacy and Politics: A Contribution to the Study of Political Right and Political Responsibility*. Cambridge: Cambridge University Press.

Compton, E. 1970. The Administrative Performance of Government. *Public Administration* 48: 3–14.

Cortés, Pablo. 2016. *The New Regulatory Framework for Consumer Dispute Resolution*. Oxford: Oxford University Press.

Cortes, P., and A.R. Lodder. 2014. Consumer Dispute Resolution Goes Online: Reflections on the Evolution of European Law for Out-of-Court Redress. *Maastricht Journal of European and Comparative Law* 1. http://papers.ssrn.com/sol3/Papers.cfm?abstract_id=2414098.

Cotterrell, Roger. 1998. Why Must Legal Ideas Be Interpreted Sociologically? *Journal of Law and Society* 25 (2): 171–192. https://doi.org/10.1111/1467-6478.00086.

Cotterell, Roger. 2005. *The Sociology of Law: An Introduction*, 2nd ed. Oxford: Oxford University Press.

Cowan, Dave. 2004. Legal Consciousness: Some Observations. *The Modern Law Review* 67 (6): 928–958.

Creutzfeldt, Naomi. 2013. The Origins and Evolution of Consumer Dispute Resolution Systems in Europe. In *Resolving Mass Disputes: ADR and Settlement of Mass Claims*, ed. C. Hodges and A. Stadler, 223–246. Cheltenham: Edward Elgar.

Creutzfeldt, Naomi. 2014. How Important Is Procedural Justice for Consumer Dispute Resolution? A Case Study of an Ombudsman Model for European Consumers. *Journal of Consumer Policy* 37 (4): 527–546.

Creutzfedt, Naomi. 2015. Alternative Dispute Resolution for Consumers. In *The Role of Consumer ADR in the Administration of Justice*, ed. M. Stuerner, F. Gascon, and R. Camponi, 3–10. Munich: Sellier.

Creutzfeldt, Naomi. 2016a. Ombudsman Schemes. In *The Transformation of Consumer Dispute Resolution in the European Union: A Renewed Approach to Consumer Protection*, ed. P. Cortes. Oxford: Oxford University Press.

Creutzfeldt, Naomi. 2016b. Implementation of the Consumer ADR Directive. *Journal of European Consumer and Market Law* 5 (4): 169–175.

Creutzfeldt, Naomi. 2016c. *Trusting the Middleman: Impact and Legitimacy of Ombudsmen in Europe—Project Report.* London: University of Westminster. Available at: https://www.law.ox.ac.uk/trusting-middle-man-impact-and-legitimacy-ombudsmen-europe/project-reports.

Creutzfeldt, Naomi. 2016d. A Voice for Change? Trust Relationships Between Ombudsmen, Individuals and Public Service Providers. *Journal of Social Welfare and Family Law* 38 (4): 460–479.

Creutzfeldt, Naomi. 2016e. What Do We Expect from an Ombudsman? Narratives of Everyday Engagement with the Informal Justice System in Germany and the UK. *International Journal of Law in Context* 12 (4): 437–452.

Creutzfeldt, Naomi. 2018. The Role of the Ombuds—A Comparative Perspective. In *Research Handbook in Comparative Law: Comparative Dispute Resolution*, ed. Maria Moscati, Michael Palmer, and Marian Roberts. Cheltenham: Edward Elgar.

Creutzfeldt, Naomi, and Ben Bradford. 2016. Dispute Resolution Outside of Courts: Procedural Justice and Decision Acceptance Among Users of Ombuds Services in the UK. *Law and Society Review* 50 (4): 985–1016.

Creutzfeldt, Naomi, and Ben Bradford. 2018. How Do Complainants Experience the Ombudsman Procedure? *Detecting Cultural Patterns of Disputing Behavior: A Comparative Analysis of Users That Complain About Financial Services.* In *Research Handbook on the Ombudsman*, ed. M. Hertogh and R. Kirkham. Cheltenham: Edward Elgar.

Creutzfeldt, Naomi and Christof Berlin. 2016. ADR in Aviation: European and National Perspectives. *Civil Justice Quarterly* 35 (2): 148–161.

Dagger, Richard. 1994. *A Culture of Rights: The Bill of Rights in Philosophy, Politics, and Law—1791 and 1991*, ed. Michael J. Lacey and Knud Haakonssen. Cambridge: Cambridge University Press: 1991, pp. viii + 474. *Utilitas* 6 (1): 157–160.

Damaška, Mirjan R. 1986. *The Faces of Justice and State Authority: A Comparative Approach to the Legal Process*. New Haven, CT: Yale University Press.

Dammer, H.R., and J.S. Albanese. 2010. *Comparative Criminal Justice Systems*, 4th ed. Belmont, CA: Wadsworth.

Denvir, David, Christopher Carman, and Robert Johns. 2012. *Elections and Voters in Britain*, 3rd ed. Basingstoke: Palgrave macmillan.

Dörrenbächer, Nora, and Ellen Mastenbroek. 2017. Passing the Buck? Analyzing the Delegation of Discretion After Transposition of European Union Law: Discretion After Transposition. *Regulation and Governance*, July. https://doi.org/10.1111/rego.12153.

Douglas, M. 1992. *Risk and Blame: Essays in Cultural Theory*. London: Routledge.

Doyle, Margaret, Varda Bondy, and Carolyn Hirst. 2014. *The Use of Informal Resolution Approaches by Ombudsmen in the UK and Ireland: A Mapping Study*. https://administrativejusticeblog.files.wordpress.com/2014/10/the-use-of-informal-resolution-approaches-by-ombudsmen-in-the-uk-and-ireland-a-mapping-study-1.pdf.

Duchesne, Sophie, and Andr´e-Paul Frognier. (1995). Is There a European Identity? In *Public Opinion and Internationalized Governance*, ed. Oskar Niedermayer and Richard Sinnott, 193–226. Oxford: Oxford University Press.

Eidenmüller, Horst. 2016a. Negotiating and Mediating Brexit, 19 October. Available at SSRN: https://papers.ssrn.com/sol3/papers.cfm?abstract_id=2854829.

Eidenmüller, Horst. 2016b. Brexit Negotiation Games. Oxford Business Law Blog, 27 June. Available at: https://www.law.ox.ac.uk/business-law-blog/blog/2016/06/brexit-negotiation-games.

Eidenmüller, Horst, and M. Engel. 2014. Against False Settlement: Designing Efficient Consumer Rights Enforcement Systems in Europe. *Ohio State Journal on Dispute Resolution* 29: 261.

Elliott, Mark, and Robert Thomas. 2012. Tribunal Justice and Proportionate Dispute Resolution. *Cambridge Law Journal* 71 (2): 297–324. Accessed 14 November 2017.

European Commission. 2011. Impact Assessment Accompanying the Document of the Proposal for a Directive on Alternative Dispute Resolution for Consumer Disputes and the Proposal for a Regulation on Online Dispute Resolution for Consumer Disputes. Staff Working Paper SEC (2011)1408.

European Commission. 2012. Memo: Alternative Dispute Resolution and Online Dispute Resolution for EU consumers: Questions and Answers. http://europa.eu/rapid/press-release_MEMO-12-994_en.htm.

Ewick, Patricia, and Susan S. Silbey. 1995. Subversive Stories and Hegemonic Tales: Toward a Sociology of Narrative. *Law & Society Review* 29 (2): 197–226.

Ewick, Patricia, and Susan S. Silbey. 1998. *The Common Place of Law: Stories from Everyday Life*. Chicago, IL: University of Chicago Press.

Falkner, Gerda, Miriam Hartlapp, Simone Leiber, and Ovoer Trieb. 2004. Non-compliance with EU-Directives: Opposition Through the Backdoor? *West European Politics* 27: 3.

Financial Ombudsman Services Annual Report 2013. http://www.financial-ombudsman.org.uk/publications/ar14/index.html.

Fisher, Roger, and William Ury. 2012. *Getting to Yes: Negotiating an Agreement Without Giving in*. London: Random House Business.

Fowler, Floyd J. 1995. *Improving Survey Questions: Design and Evaluation*. London: Sage.

Fox, Kate. 2014. *Watching the English: The International Bestseller Revised and Updated*. London: Hodder & Stoughton.

Friedman, Lawrence M. 1969. Legal Culture and Social Development. *Law and Society Review* 4 (1): 29–44.

Fritzvold, E. 2009. Under the Law: Legal Consciousness and Radical Environmental Activism. *Law & Social Inquiry* 34 (4): 799–824.

Geddes, Mike. 2000. Tackling Social Exclusion in the European Union? The Limits to the New Orthodoxy of Local Partnership. *International Journal of Urban and Regional Research* 24 (4): 782–800. Accessed 14 November 2017.

Genn, H. 1993. Tribunals and Informal Justice. *Modern Law Review* 56 (3): 399–411.

Genn, H. 2010. *Judging Civil Justice*. Cambridge: Cambridge University Press.

Genn, H. 2012. What Is Civil Justice for-Reform, ADR, and Access to Justice. *Yale Journal of Law and Humanity* 24: 397.

Genn, H., and S. Beinart. 1999. *Paths to Justice: What People Do and Think About Going to Law*. Oxford: Hart.

Gibson, B., and P. Cavadino. 2008. *The Criminal Justice System: An Introduction*, revised/updated ed. Winchester: Waterside Press.

Gilad, Sharon. 2008. Accountability or Expectations Management? The Role of the Ombudsman in Financial Regulation. *Law and Policy* 30 (2): 227–253.

Gill, Chris. 2011. Right First Time: The Role of Ombudsmen in Influencing Administrative Decision-Making. *Journal of Social Welfare and Family Law* 33: 181–192.

Gill, Chris, and Naomi Creutzfeldt. 2017. The "Ombuds Watchers": Dissatisfaction, Collective Dissent, and Legal Protest Amongst Users of Public Service Ombuds. *Social & Legal Studies*. http://journals.sagepub.com/doi/abs/10.1177/0964663917721313.

Gill, Chris, Naomi Creutzfeldt, Jane Williams, Sarah O'Neill, and N. Vivian. 2017. *Confusion, Gaps, and Overlaps: A Consumer Perspective on Alternative Dispute Resolution Between Consumers and Businesses*. http://westminsterresearch.wmin.ac.uk/18948/.

Goldberg, S.B., F.E.A. Sander, N.H. Rogers, and S.R. Cole. 2012. *Dispute Resolution: Negotiation, Mediation, Arbitration, and Other Processes*, 6th ed. New York: Wolters Kluwer.

Gomes, Ana Sofia. 2015. The proposal for a Regulation on a Common European Sales Law (CESL): An Introduction. *European Perspectives on the Common European Sales Law*, 1–15. Studies in European Economic Law and Regulation. Cham: Springer. https://doi.org/10.1007/978-3-319-10497-3_1.

Greenberg, J., and R. Folger. 1983. Procedural Justice Participation and the Pair Process Effect in Groups and Organizations. In *Basic Group Processes*, ed. P.B. Paulus, 235–256. New York: Springer-Verlag.

Greenberg, J., and T.R. Tyler. 1987. Why Study Procedural Justice in Organizations? *Social Justice Research* 1 (2): 127–142.

Groves, M. 2017. *Legitimate Expectations in the Common Law World*, ed. Greg Weeks. Oxford: Hart.

Guardian. 2011. Access to Justice is a Fine Concept, but What Does It Mean in View of Cuts to Legal Aid? https://www.theguardian.com/law/2011/oct/06/access-to-justice-legal-aid-cuts.

Gulland, J. 2010. Current Developments in the UK—Complaints Procedures and Ombudsmen. In *Administrative Justice in Context*, ed. M. Adler. Oxford: Hart.

Habermas, Jürgen. 1994. Three Normative Models of Democracy. *Constellations* 1 (1): 1–10.

Habermas, Jürgen. 1996. *Between Facts and Norms: Contributions to a Discourse Theory of Law and Democracy*. Cambridge: Polity Press.

Halliday, Simon, and Bronwen Morgan. 2013. I Fought the Law and the Law Won? Legal Consciousness and the Critical Imagination. *Current Legal Problems* 66 (1): 1–32.

Harlow, Carol, and Richard Rawlings. 1984. *Law and Administration*. London: Weidenfield and Nicolson.

Harlow, Carol, and Richard Rawlings. 2009. *Law and Administration*, 3rd ed. Cambridge, UK and New York: Cambridge University Press.

Hawdon, J. 2008. Legitimacy, Trust, Social Capital, and Policing Styles: A Theoretical Statement. *Police Quarterly* 11 (2): 182–201.

Head, J.W. 2011. *Great Legal Traditions: Civil Law, Common Law, and Chinese Law in Historical and Operational Perspective*. Durham, NC: Carolina Academic Press.

Heede, Katja. 2000. *European Ombudsman: Redress and Control at Union Level*. Hague, London and Boston: Kluwer Law International.

Herrmann, Richard K., Thomas Risse-Kappen, and Marilynn B. Brewer. 2004. *Transnational Identities: Becoming European in the EU*. Lanham, MD: Rowman & Littlefield.

Hertogh, Marc, and Marina Kurkchiyan. 2016. 'When Politics Comes into Play, Law Is No Longer Law': Images of Collective Legal Consciousness in the UK, Poland and Bulgaria. *International Journal of Law in Context* 12 (4): 404–419.

Hirsch, Günter. 2013. The Ombudsman in Germany. Speech Mumbai, October 2013. http://www.emergingmarketsdialogue.org/dms/giz-emd/events/event2/

Session-5-Speaker-1-Prof.Dr.-Hirsch-Ombudsman-in-Germany/Session%20 5%20Speaker%201%20Prof.Dr.%20Hirsch%20Ombudsman%20in%20 Germany.pdf.

Hodges, Christopher, Iris Benöhr, and Naomi Creutzfeldt-Banda. 2012a. *Consumer ADR in Europe*. Oxford: Hart.

Hodges, Christopher, Iris Benöhr, and Naomi Creutzfeldt-Banda. 2012b. Consumer-to-Business Dispute Resolution: The Power of CADR. *ERA Forum* 13 (2): 199–225. Accessed 14 November 2017. https://doi.org/10.1007/s12027-012-0263-y.

Hoffmann, Elizabeth A. 2003. Legal Consciousness and Dispute Resolution: Different Disputing Behavior at Two Similar Taxicab Companies. *Law & Social Inquiry* 28 (3): 691–716.

Hofstede, Geert. 1980. *Culture's Consequences—International Differences in Work-Related Values*. Beverly Hills, CA: Sage.

Hofstede, Geert. 2001. *Culture's Consequences: Comparing Values, Behaviors, Institutions, and Organizations Across Nations*. London: Sage. http://digitalcommons.usu.edu/unf_research/53.

Höland, Armin, and Caroline Meller-Hannich. 2017. *Nichts zu klagen? Der Rückgang der Klageeingangszahlen in der Justiz.Mögliche Ursachen und Folgen*. Baden-Baden.

Hopt, Klaus J., and Felix Steffek (eds.). 2012. *Mediation: Principles and Regulation in Comparative Perspective*. Oxford: Oxford University Press.

Hough, Mike, and Mai Sato. 2011. *Trust in Justice: Why It Is Important for Criminal Policy, and How It Can Be Measured: Final Report of the Euro-Justis Project*. Helsinki: European Institute for Crime Prevention and Control, affiliated with the United Nations (HEUNI).

Hough, Mike, and Tom R. Tyler. 2015. Why Do People Comply with the Law? Legitimacy and the Influence of Legal Institutions. *British Journal of Criminology* 52 (6): 1051–1071.

Hough, Mike, Jonathan Jackson, and Ben Bradford. 2013a. Legitimacy, Trust and Compliance: An Empirical Test of Procedural Justice Theory Using the European Social Survey. New Haven, CT: Yale University Press. https://www.researchgate.net/publication/235983477_Legitimacy_Trust_And_Compliance_An_Empirical_Test_Of_Procedural_Justice_Theory_Using_The_European_Social_Survey.

Hough, Mike, Jonathan Jackson, and Ben Bradford. 2013b. Legitimacy, Trust and Compliance: An Empirical Test of Procedural Justice Theory Using the European Social Survey. http://papers.ssrn.com/sol3/papers.cfm?abstract_id=2234339.

Hyman, Herbert Hiram. 1959. *Political Socialization: A Study in the Psychology of Political Behavior*. New York: Free Press.

Jackson, Jonathan, Ben Bradford, Mike Hough, Jouni Kuha, Sally Stares, Sally Widdop, Rory Fitzgerald, Maria Yordanova, and Todor Galev. 2011. Developing European Indicators of Trust in Justice. *European Journal of Criminology* 8 (4): 267–285.

Jackson, Jonathan, Ben Bradford, Betsy Stanko, and Katrin Hohl. 2012. *Just Authority? Trust in the Police in England and Wales*. London: Routledge.

Jackson, Jonathan, and Jacinta M. Gau. 2016. Carving Up Concepts? Differentiating Between Trust and Legitimacy in Public Attitudes Towards Legal Authority. In *Interdisciplinary Perspectives on Trust*, ed. Ellie Shockley, Tess M.S. Neal, Lisa M. Pytlik Zillig, and Brian H. Bornstein, 49–69. Cham: Springer International.

Jackson, Jonathan, Jouni Kuha, Mike Hough, Ben Bradford, Katrin Hohl, and Monica M. Gerber. 2013. Trust and Legitimacy Across EUROPE: A FIDUCIA Report on Comparative Public Attitudes Towards Legal Authority. SSRN Scholarly Paper ID 2272975.

Jackson, Jonathan, Mike Hough, B. Bradford, K. Hohl Pooler, and J. Kuha. 2011. *Trust in Justice: Topline Results from Round 5 of the European Social Survey*. Brussels: European Commission.

Jackson, Sir Rupert. (2016). Civil Justice Reform and Alternative Dispute Resolution. Lecture to the Chartered Institute of Arbitrators. Accessed 14 November 2017. http://www.ciarb.org/docs/defaultsource/ciarbdocuments/events/papers/lord_jackson_speech_200916.pdf?sfvrsn=0.

Jacobsson, K. 2004. Between Deliberation and Discipline: Soft Governance in EU Employment Policy. In *Soft Law and Governance and Regulation: An Interdisciplinary Analysis*, ed. U. Mörth. Cheltenham: Edward Elgar.

Jones, Peter, and Ian O'Flynn. 2013. Can a Compromise Be Fair? *Politics, Philosophy and Economics* 12 (2): 115–135. https://doi.org/10.1177/1470594X12447773.

Jowell, Sir Jeffrey, and Dawn Oliver (eds.). 2007. *The Changing Constitution*, 6th ed. Oxford and New York: Oxford University Press.

Kaeding, Michael, and Friederike Voskamp. 2011. Better Implementation of EU Legislation Is Not Just a Question of Taking Member States to Court. EIPA Working Paper 2011/W/01. European Institute of Public Administration, Maastricht. Accessed 14 November 2017. http://www.eipa.eu/files/repository/product/20120228091739_Workingpaper2011_W_01.pdf.

Kaiser, Kimberly A. 2016. Procedural Justice and Legal Socialization Among Serious Adolescent Offenders: A Longitudinal Examination. Arizona State University. http://search.proquest.com/openview/ce3ed1558af1d97608f7f8a5896e5036/1?pq-origsite=gscholar&cbl=18750&diss=y.

Katsh, Ethan, Janet Rifkin, and Alan Gaitenby. 1999. E-Commerce, E-Disputes, and E-Dispute Resolution: In the Shadow of eBay Law. *Ohio State Journal on Dispute Resolution* 15 (3): 705–734.

Katsh, Ethan, and Orna Rabinovich-Einy. 2017. *Digital Justice: Technology and the Internet of Disputes*. New York: Oxford University Press.

Kirkham, Richard. 2005. A Complainant's View of the Local Government Ombudsman. *Journal of Social Welfare and Family Law* 27 (3–4): 383–394.

Kirkham, Richard. 2016. The Ombudsman, Tribunals and Administrative Justice Section: A 2020 Vision for the Ombudsman Sector. *Journal of Social Welfare and Family Law* 38 (1): 103–114.

Koch, Insa. 2016. Bread-and-Butter Politics: Democratic Disenchantment and Everyday Politics on an English Council Estate. *American Ethnologist* 43 (2): 282–294.

Kohler-Koch, Beate. 2003. *Linking EU and National Governance*. Oxford: Oxford University Press.

Kucsko-Stadlmayer, Gabriele. 2009. The Spread of the Ombudsman Idea in Europe. *International Ombudsman Institute Paper*. http://www.theioi.org/downloads/34chi/Stockholm%20Conference_25.%20Back%20o%20the%20Roots_Gabriele%20Kucsko%20Stadlmayer.pdf.

Laffan, Brigid. 1996. The Politics of Identity and Political Order in Europe. *Journal of Common Market Studies* 34 (1): 81–103.

Legrand, Pierre. 1997. The Impossibility of "Legal Transplants". *Maastricht Journal of European and Comparative Law* 4 (2): 111.

Lazarus, Liora. 2004. *Contrasting Prisoners' Rights: A Comparative Examination of England and Germany*. Oxford Monographs on Criminal Law and Justice. Oxford and New York: Oxford University Press.

Lens, Vicki. 2007. In the Fair Hearing Room: Resistance and Confrontation in the Welfare Bureaucracy. *Law & Social Inquiry* 32 (2): 309–332.

Leung, K., and A. Lind. 1986. Procedural Justice and Culture: Effects of Culture, Gender, and Investigator Status on Procedural Preferences. *Journal of Personality and Social Psychology* 50 (6): 1134–1140.

Levine, Kay, and Virginia Mellema. 2001. Strategizing the Street: How Law Matters in the Lives of Women in the Street-Level Drug Economy. *Law and Social Inquiry* 26 (1): 169–207.

Lewis, X. 1995. A Common Law Fortress Under Attack: Is English Law Being Europeanized? *Columbia Journal of European Law* 2: 1.

Lind, E.A. 1994. Procedural Justice and Culture: Evidence for Ubiquitous Process Concerns. *Zeitschrififiir Rechtssoziologie* 15: 24–36.

Lind, E.A. 1995. *Social Conflict and Social Justice: Some Lessons from the Social Psychology of Justice*. Leiden: Leiden University Press.

Lind, E.A., and P. Christopher Earley. 1992. Procedural Justice and Culture. *International Journal of Psychology* 27 (2): 227–242.

Lind, E.A., and Tom R. Tyler. 1988. *The Social Psychology of Procedural Justice*. New York: Springer.

Lind, E.A., S. Kurtz, L. Musante, L. Walker, and J. Thibaut. 1980. Procedure and Outcome Effects on Reactions to Adjudicated Resolution of Conflicts of Interests. *Journal of Personality and Social Psychology* 39: 643–653.

Lind, E.A., R.J. MacCoun, P.A. Ebener, W.L.F. Felstiner, D.R. Hensler, J. Resnik, and T.R. Tyler. 1990. In the Eye of the Beholder: Tort Litigants Evaluations of Civil Justice System Experiences. *Law and Society Review* 24: 953–996.

Loughlin, Martin. 1992. *Public Law and Political Theory*. Oxford: Clarendon Press.

Louin-Tapp, June. 1991. The Geography of Legal Socialization: Scientific and Social Markers. *Droit et Société* 19 (1): 329–353.

Mair, Jane. 2017. Lawyers and Mediators: The Brave New World of Services for Separating Families. *Journal of Social Welfare and Family Law* 39 (1): 137–139.

Marsden, Christopher T. 2011. *Internet Co-regulation: European Law, Regulatory Governance and Legitimacy in Cyberspace*. Cambridge: Cambridege University Press.

Marshall, Anna-Maria. 2006. Communities and Culture: Enriching Legal Consciousness and Legal Culture. *Law and Social Inquiry* 31 (1): 229–249.

Martinotti, Guido, and Sonia Stefanizzi. 1998. Europeans and the Nation state. In *Public Opinion and Internationalized Governance*, ed. Oskar Niedermayer and Richard Sinnott. Oxford: Oxford University Press.

Mashaw, J. 1983. *Bureaucratic Justice: Managing Social Security Disability Claims*. New Haven, CT: Yale University Press.

Mauss, M. 1995. 'Essai sur le don', Sociologie et Anthropologie 6 (Originally published in 1925). Paris: Presses Universitaires de France.

Menkel-Meadow, Carrie. 2003. *Dispute Processing and Conflict Resolution: Theory, Practice, and Policy*. Burlington, VT: Ashgate.

Menkel-Meadow, Carrie. 2004. From Legal Disputes to Conflict Resolution and Human Problem Solving: Legal Dispute Resolution in a Multidisciplinary Context. *Journal of Legal Education* 54 (1): 7–29.

Menkel-Meadow, Carrie. 2005. Peace and Justice: Notes on the Evolution and Purposes of Legal Processes. *Georgtown Law Journal* 94: 553–580.

Menkel-Meadow, Carrie. 2010. Empirical Studies of ADR: The Baseline Problem of What ADR is and What it is Compared to. In *Oxford Handbook of Empirical Legal Studies*, ed. Peter Cane and Herbert Kritzer. Oxford: Oxford University Press. http://papers.ssrn.com/sol3/papers.cfm?abstract_id=1485563.

Menkel-Meadow, Carrie. 2013. Regulation of Dispute Resolution in the United States of America: From the Formal to the Informal to the "Semi-formal". In *Regulating Dispute Resolution: ADR and Access to Justice at the Crossroads*, ed. Felix Steffek, Hannes Unberath, Hazel Genn, Reinhard Greger, and Carrie Menkel-Meadow. Oxford: Hart.

Menkel-Meadow, Carrie. 2014. Alternative/Appropriate Dispute Resolution in Context: Informal, Formal and Semi-formal Legal Processes. In *Handbook of Conflict Resolution*, 3rd ed., ed. Peter Coleman and Morton Deutsch. San Fransisco: Jossey Bass Wiley.

Menkel-Meadow, Carrie. 2015. Process Pluralism in Transitional/Restorative Justice—Lessons from Dispute Resolution for Cultural Variations in Goals beyond Rule of Law and Democracy Development (Argentina and Chile). *International Journal of Conflict Engagement and Resolution* 3 (1). UC Irvine School of Law Research Paper No. 2015–86. https://ssrn.com/abstract=2683501.

Menkel-Meadow, Carrie. 2016a. Blogpost: The History and Development of "A" DR (alternative/appropriate dispute resolution). http://voelkerrechtsblog.org/the-history-and-development-of-a-dr-alternativeappropriate-dispute-resolution/.

Menkel-Meadow, Carrie. 2016b. Is ODR ADR? Reflections of an ADR Founder from 15th ODR Conference, 13 May. Accessed 14 November 2017. https://law-tech-a2j.org/odr/is-odr-adr-reflections-of-an-adr-founder-from-15th-odr-conference/.

Merry, Sally Engle. 1985. Concepts of Law and Justice Among Working-Class Americans: Ideology as Culture. *Legal Studies Forum* 9 (1): 59–69.

Merry, Sally Engle. 1987. Disputing Without Culture. *Harvard Law Review* 100 (8): 2057–2073.

Merry, Sally Engle. 1990. *Getting Justice and Getting Even: Legal Consciousness Among Working-Class Americans*. Chicago: University of Chicago Press.

Mill, John Stuart. 1950. *John Stuart Mill's Philosophy of Scientific Method*. New york: University of Michigan, Hafner.

Möllering, Guido. 2006. *Trust: Reason, Routine, Reflexivity*. Bingley: Emerald.

Morgan, Bronwen, and Declan Kuch. 2015. Radical Transactionalism: Legal Consciousness, Diverse Economies, and the Sharing Economy. *Journal of Law and Society* 42 (4): 556–587.

Mullen, Tom. 2010. A Holistic Approach to Administrative Justice? In *Administrative Justice in Context*, ed. Michael Adler, 383–420. Oxford: Hart.

Murphy, Kristina, Tom R. Tyler, and Amy Curtis. 2009. Nurturing Regulatory Compliance: Is Procedural Justice Effective When People Question the Legitimacy of the Law? *Regulation & Governance* 3 (1): 1–26.

Nelken, David. 2004. Using the Concept of Legal Culture. *Australian Journal of Legal Philosophy* 29: 1–26.

Nelken, David. 2013. Comparative Sociology of Law. In *Law and Social Theory*, ed. R. Banakar, and M. Travers. Oxford: Hart.

Neuberger, Lord. 2017. Access to Justice: Welcome Address to Australian Bar Association Biennial Conference, 3 July, London and Dublin.

Norrie, Alan. 1996. From Law to Popular Justice: Beyond Antinomialism. *Social and Legal Studies* 5 (3): 383–404.

O'Brien, Nick. 2002. Ombudsmen and the Courts: Time for Dialogue. *The Ombudsman*, December.

O'Brien, Nick. 2015a. *A Democratic Alternative*. UK Administrative Justice Institute. https://ukaji.org/2015/10/08/a-democratic-alternative.

O'Brien, Nick. 2015b. What Future for the Ombudsman? *Political Quarterly* 86 (1): 72–80.

O'Neill, Onora. 2002. *A Question of Trust: The BBC Reith Lectures 2002*. Cambridge, UK: Cambridge University Press. http://assets.cambridge.org/97805215/29969/sample/9780521529969ws.pdf.

Ombudsman Services. 2017. Making a Difference Together. Accessed 14 November 2017. https://www.ombudsman-services.org/docs/default-source/annual-reports/os-report-2016.pdf?sfvrsn=4.

Paris Innovation Review. 2017. Predictive Justice: When Algorithms Pervade the Law. Accessed 14 November 2017. http://parisinnovationreview.com/articles-en/predictive-justice-when-algorithms-pervade-the-law.

Parliamentary and Health Services Ombudsman Annual Report. 2013. *A Voice or Change.* https://www.ombudsman.org.uk/sites/default/files/2016-10/Annual%20 Report%202013-14.pdf.

Pound, Roscoe. 1906. Causes of Popular Dissatisfaction with the Administration of Justice. *American Law Review* 40: 729.

Pound, Roscoe. 1938. *The Formative Era of American Law.* London: Little, Brown & Co.

Pound, Roscoe. 1999. *The Spirit of the Common Law.* New Brunswick, NJ: Transaction.

Power Inquiry (Great Britain), and Joseph Rowntree Foundation. 2007. *Power to the People: The Report of Power: An Independent Inquiry into Britain's Democracy.* York: Joseph Rowntree Charitable Trust, Power Inquiry. http://www.jrrt.org.uk/sites/jrrt.org.uk/files/documents/PowertothePeople_001.pdf.

Puchalska-Tych, Bogumila, and Michael Salter. 1996. Comparing Legal Cultures of Eastern Europe: The Need for a Dialectical Analysis. *Legal Studies* 16 (2): 157–184.

Rabinovich-Einy, Orna. 2006. Technology's Impact: The Quest for a New Paradigm for Accountability in Mediation. *Harvard Negotiation Law Review* 11: 253–293.

Rawls, John. 1999. *A Theory of Justice*, rev. ed. Cambridge, MA: Harvard University Press.

Reif, Linda C. 2004. *The Ombudsman, Good Governance, and the International Human Rights System.* Leiden: Martinus Nijhoff Publishers.

Reif, Linda C. 2013. *The Ombudsman, Good Governance and the International Human Rights System.* New York: Springer.

Renshon, Stanley Allen. 1977. *Handbook of Political Socialization: Theory and Research.* New York: Free Press.

Risse, Thomas. 2010. *A Community of Europeans?: Transnational Identities and Public Spheres.* Ithaca: Cornell University Press.

Roberts, M., and M. Palmer. 2005. *Dispute Processes*, 2nd ed. Cambridge: Cambridge University Press.

Robins, Jon. 2011. Access to Justice Is a Fine Concept, but What Does It Mean in View of Cuts to Legal Aid? *The Guardian*, October 5. Accessed 14 November 2017. http://www.theguardian.com/law/2011/oct/06/access-to-justice-legal-aid-cuts.

Rosamond, B. 2000. *Theories of European Integration.* Hampshire: Palgrave Macmillan.

Rosen, L. 2008. *Law as Culture.* Princeton, NJ: Princeton University Press. http://press.princeton.edu/titles/8179.html.

Rowat, Donald. 2007. The American Distortion of the Ombudsman Concept and Its Influence on Canada. *Canadian Public Administration* 50 (1): 42–52.

Rowe, Mary, and Howard Gadlin. 2014. The Organizational Ombudsman. In *The Oxford Handbook of Conflict Management in Organizations*, 210. Oxford: Oxford University Press.

Sander, Frank E.A., and Stephen B. Goldberg. 1994. Fitting the Forum to the Fuss: A User-Friendly Guide to Selecting an ADR Procedure. *Negotiation Journal* 10 (1): 49–68.

Sarat, A., and B.G. Garth. 1998. *How Does Law Matter? Fundamental Issues in Law and Society*. Evanston, IL: Northwestern University Press.

Schuerkens, Ulrike. 2003. The Sociological and Anthropological Study of Globalization and Localization. *Current Sociology* 51 (3–4): 209–222. Accessed 14 November 2017. https://doi.org/10.1177/0011392103051003004.

Schulte-Nölke, Hans. 2015. The Brave New World of EU Consumer Law: Without Consumers, or Even Without Law? *Journal of EU Consumer and Market Law* 4: 135–139.

Schwartz, David G. 2005. Regulation and the Internet. *Internet Research* 15 (4). Accessed 14 November 2017. https://doi.org/10.1108/intr.2005.17215daa.001.

Seneviratne, M. 2002. *Ombudsmen: Public Services and Administrative Justice*. London: Butterworths LexisNexis.

Seneviratne, M. 2005. Researching Ombudsmen. In *Theory and Method in Socio-Legal Research*, ed. Reza Banakar and Max Travers. Oxford: Hart.

Silbey, Susan S. 2005. After Legal Consciousness. *Annual Review of Law and Social Science* 1 (1): 323–368. https://doi.org/10.1146/annurev.lawsocsci.1.041604.115938.

Silbey, Susan S. 2010. Legal Culture and Cultures of Legality. In *Sociology of Culture: A Handbook*, ed. John R. Hall, Laura Grindstaff, and Ming-Cheng Lo, 470–479. London: Routledge.

Stefan Wrbka, S. 2015. *European Consumer Access to Justice Revisited*. Cambridge, UK and New York: Cambridge University Press.

Stein, P. 1992. Roman Law, Common Law, and Civil Law. *Tulane Law Review* 66: 1591.

Sternlight, J.R. 2003. ADR Is Here: Preliminary Reflections on Where It Fits in a System of Justice. *Scholarly Works* 289–304.

Stipanowich, T.J. 2004. ADR and the 'Vanishing Trial': The Growth and Impact of 'Alternative Dispute Resolution'. *Journal of Empirical Legal Studies* 1 (3): 843–912. Accessed 14 November 2017. http://papers.ssrn.com/sol3/papers.cfm?abstract_id=1380922.

Strassoldo, Raimondo. 1992. Globalism and Localism: Theoretical Reflections and Some Evidence. In *Globalisation and Territorial Identities*, ed. Zdravko Mlinar, 35–59. Aldershot: Avebury.

Sunshine, Jason, and Tom R. Tyler. 2003. The Role of Procedural Justice and Legitimacy in Shaping Public Support for Policing. *Law & Society Review* 37 (3): 513–548.

Susskind, Richard, and Daniel Susskind. 2015. *The Future of the Professions: How Technology Will Transform the Work of Human Experts*. Oxford: Oxford University Publisher.

Tankebe, Justice. 2009. Public Cooperation with the Police in Ghana: Does Procedural Fairness Matter? *Criminology* 47 (4): 1265–1293.

Tapp, June Louin, and L. Kohlberg. 1971. Developing Senses of Law and Legal Justice. *Journal of Social Issues* 27 (2): 65–91.

Tapp, June Louin, and Felice J. Levine. 1974. Legal Socialization: Strategies for an Ethical Legality. *Stanford Law Review* 27 (1): 1–72.

Thibaut, J., and L. Walker. 1975. *Procedural Justice: A Psychological Analsysis*. Hillsdale, NJ: Laurence Erlbaum Associates.

Trinkner, Rick, and Ellen S. Cohn. 2014. Putting the "Social" Back in Legal Socialization: Procedural Justice, Legitimacy, and Cynicism in Legal and Nonlegal Authorities. *Law and Human Behavior* 38 (6): 602–617.

Trinkner, Rick, and Tom R. Tyler. 2016. Legal Socialization: Coercion Versus Consent in an Era of Mistrust. *Annual Review of Law and Social Science* 12: 417–439.

Trubek, D., and L. Trubek. 2005. Hard and Soft Law in the Construction of Social Europe: The Role of the Open Method of Coordination. *European Law Journal* 11: 343–364.

Tyler, Tom R. 1988. What is Procedural Justice?: Criteria Used by Citizens to Assess the Fairness of Legal Procedures. *Law and Society Review* 22: 103–135.

Tyler, Tom R. 1989. The Quality of Dispute Resolution Processes and Outcomes: Measurement Problems and Possibilities. *Denver University Law Review* 66: 419–436.

Tyler, Tom R. 1994. Governing Amid Diversity: The Effect of Fair Decision-Making Procedures on the Legitimacy of Government. *Law and Society Review* 28: 809–831.

Tyler, Tom R. 1996. The Relationship of the Outcome and Procedural Fairness: How does Knowing the Outcome Influence Judgments About the Procedure? *Social Justice Research* 9 (4): 311–325.

Tyler, Tom R. 2003. Procedural Justice, Legitimacy, and the Effective Rule of Law. *Crime and Justice* 30 (January): 283–357.

Tyler, Tom R. 2006. *Why People Obey the Law*. Princeton, NJ: Princeton University Press.

Tyler, Tom R. 2009. Legitimacy and Criminal Justice: The Benefits of Self-regulation. *Ohio State Journal of Criminal Law* 7: 307–359.

Tyler, Tom R., and A. Caine. 1981. The Role of Distributional and Procedural Fairness in the Endorsement of Formal Leaders. *Journal of Personality and Social Psychology* 41: 642–655.

Tyler, Tom R., and R. Folger. 1980. Distributional and Procedural Aspects of Satisfaction with Citizen-Police Encounters. *Basic and Applied Social Psychology* 1: 281–292.

Tyler, Tom R., and Kenneth Rasinski. 1991. Procedural Justice, Institutional Legitimacy, and the Acceptance of Unpopular US Supreme Court Decisions: A Reply to Gibson. *Law and Society Review* 25 (3): 621–629.

Tyler, Tom R., and Heather Smith. 1999. Justice, Social Identity, and Group Processes. In *The Psychology of the Social Self*, ed. Tom R. Tyler, Roderick M. Kramer, and Oliver P. John. Routledge: Psychology Press.

Tyler, Tom R., and Steven L. Blader. 2000. *Cooperation in Groups: Procedural Justice, Social Identity, and Behavioral Engagement*. Hove: Psychology Press.

Tyler, Tom R., and Yuen J. Huo. 2002. *Trust in the Law: Encouraging Public Cooperation with the Police and Courts*. New York: Russell Sage Foundation.

Unlock the Law. 2015. Justice Online: Online Courts for Smaller Claims and Online UK Legal Help. Accessed 14 November 2017. https://www.unlockthelaw.co.uk/News/online-courts-for-smaller-claims-uk/365794092.html.

Ury, W.L., J.M. Brett, and S.B. Goldberg. 1988. Designing an Effective Dispute Resolution System. *Negotiation Journal* 4 (4): 413–431.

Van den Bos, Kees, and E.A. Lind. 2002. Uncertainty Management by Means of Fairness Judgments. *Advances in Experimental Social Psychology* 34: 1–60.

Van den Bos, Kees, and Riël Vermunt. 1997. Procedural and Distributive Justice: What Is Fair Depends More on What Comes First Than on What Comes Next. *Journal of Personality and Social Psychology* 72 (1): 95–104.

Vidmar, Neil. 1992. Commentary: Procedural Justice and Alternative Dispute Resolution. *Psychological Science* 3 (4): 224–228.

Watson, Alan. 1993. *Legal Transplants: An Approach to Comparative Law*, 2nd ed. Athens: University of Georgia Press.

Wells, H. 2008. The Techno-Fix Versus The Fair Cop: Procedural (In)Justice and Automated Speed Limit Enforcement. *British Journal of Criminology* 48 (6): 798–817.

Welsh, Nancy A. 2002. 'Disputants' Decision Control in Court-Connected Mediation: A Hollow Promise Without Procedural Justice. *Journal of Dispute Resolution*, 1: 179–192.

Wiener, A., and T. Diez (eds.). 2004. *European Integration Theory*. Oxford: Oxford University Press.

Wilk, Richard. 1995. Learning to Be Local in Belize: Global Systems of Common Difference. In *Worlds Apart*, ed. D. Miler, 110–133. New York: Routledge.

Wojkowska, Ewa. 2006. *How Informal Justice Systems Can Contribute*. Oslo, United Nations. http://www.eldis.org/vfile/upload/1/document/1201/UNDP%20DoingJusticeEwaWojkowska130307.pdf.

Wranken, Martin. 2015. *Western Legal Traditions: A comparison of Civil and Common Law*. Annandale, NSW: Federation Press.

Wrbka, S. 2014. *European Consumer Access to Justice Revisited*. Cambridge: Cambridge University Press.

Zedner, L. 2004. *Criminal Justice*. Oxford: Oxford University Press.

Index

N. Creutzfeldt, *Ombudsmen and ADR*, Palgrave Socio-Legal Studies,
https://doi.org/10.1007/978-3-319-78807-4

The manufacturer's authorised representative in the EU is Springer Nature Customer Service Centre GmbH, Europaplatz 3, 69115 Heidelberg, Germany. If you have any concerns regarding our products, please contact ProductSafety@springernature.com

Printed and bound by CPI Group (UK) Ltd, Croydon, CR0 4YY
05/10/2026
02228128-0018